DESIGN FOR FAMILY LIVING

DEVOTIONS FOR FAMILIES WITH TEEN-AGERS

BY ROY BLUMHORST

CONCORDIA PUBLISHING HOUSE

SAINT LOUIS

INTRODUCTION

One of the worst blows we can deal to the Christian faith
is to elevate it to irrelevance. We do this when we turn it
into great truths and feel that in holding these truths with
precision we are being Christian. The early Christians called
themselves adherents of "the Way." They knew they were
committed to a pattern of life completely dominated by the
Lord Jesus Christ and that this pattern included every aspect
of their daily lives.

No finer example of this conviction can be seen than
the Letter of James. To be sure, those who do not like to
think of Christianity in such all-inclusive terms have found
James a severe book, one full of "Law" instead of the joyful
news about salvation. But they are so wrong! James is so
convinced of the good news that his letter brings it into
every aspect of life. He simply takes seriously our statement
that Jesus is Lord, and he brings this to bear on all of life.

The Christian family realizes that Jesus is Lord. Its
hopes, its goals, its problems all revolve around Him. So
James. He sees even the little problems and the minor
irritations that are so typical of family living. He brings
the great message of the Gospel to bear on these little
daily matters.

This book endeavors to lead a Christian family through
the message of James. The writer has in mind chiefly
a family with teen-age members, but others may easily
adapt it to their situation. The author thinks of a family
sitting down together to read the section of James and the

short meditation. This leads to a discussion on the basis of the questions given. We don't look for "right answers" to the questions. The questions are rather to help us take an honest look at ourselves and to bring the message right into the family circle. As this is done, the family will be challenged to live as a little congregation, a group of fellow Christians hearing, helping, forgiving one another. Real value will result when Father and Mother can converse with teen-agers in a setting which permits them to express their doubts and to discuss their problems about specific sins. Such a conversation will help them share the power of the Holy Spirit.

Such conversations of Christians lead to prayer, the response of God's people to His Word and their expression of concern for one another. It is hoped that the family will go beyond the brief prayer suggestions.

The meditations are based on J. B. Phillips' translation instead of the familiar King James Version of 1611. No other translation speaks so clearly in the present-day English idiom and captures so well the urgency and practicality with which James addresses his readers. Other quotations from Scripture, however, may be from the KJV or the RSV.

Prepare to embark on a joyful journey through James. The author can assure a joyful trip, not because he has done anything to guarantee it but because he so thoroughly enjoyed the experience when he set out on it.

Scattered Christians

James, servant of God and of the Lord Jesus Christ, sends greeting to the twelve dispersed tribes. James 1:1

"Dispersed" is the word for what happened to the twelve tribes of Israel in their crushing defeat by the big countries to the northeast. They were scattered over the world.

"Dispersed" is the word for what happened to the first Christians under the heavy hand of Herod too. They were driven away from Jerusalem to cities everywhere.

And "scattered" is often the way we Christians look in the twentieth century. The New Testament calls us the "body of Christ," but we don't look like a body sometimes. We wonder if any of the other people at high school are concerned about living the life in Christ. We usually assume this is a private matter. And speaking of private matters, how about the office? A man's faith frequently seems relegated to a private affair in our workaday world. Even looking at our little neighborhood often makes us feel like a few scattered Christians in an otherwise uninterested world.

The trouble with being scattered is that it can take away a great deal of our strength. When I am the only one in the crowd who cares about Christ, it can be pretty hard to "let my light shine." If I seem to be the only believer, there are plenty of times when I wonder about my faith too. So being scattered isn't good if it causes Christians to feel defeated or deserted most of the time.

That's why it should come as good news to us that we are not scattered at all. Can you imagine the French underground in World War II? Just to look at them, people would say the French were completely crushed as they floundered under the occupation forces. But under the surface was an extremely close-knit group of people who were working toward that common goal, the liberation of France. Step below the surface and you saw perhaps the most united group in the world.

So we step below the surface and take a good look at the Christian church. Men may be scattered, but a grand movement to unity has begun. The source of the scattering is the rebellion, sin, and evil of the world. The spearhead of the unity is the Lord Jesus Christ, who reunites men with God again and in that reunion brings men back together. So there is a powerful bond between us though we may be scattered throughout schools, offices, churches. The bond is our oneness in our Lord Christ.

The only real problem is to bring this unity to the surface and thrive on the strength we already have. We need to listen to one another, pray with one another, encourage one another often so we can go back to our places in life with renewed strength.

Our family can be one of these sources of strength. We don't have to confine ourselves to Sunday morning for mutual support. We have right here a clustering of those who are in Christ Jesus.

So let's talk for a moment:

What kind of family member do I make?

Is it easy in our family to speak about Christ and what He means to us?

Is ours a forgiving and strengthening family?

How can our family give more opportunity for "Christian conversation"?

You might want to close with this prayer:

We thank You, heavenly Father, for making us a family together and joining us in Jesus Christ. Let Your Holy Spirit live in us to hold us together and make us strong, to Your glory.

In Training

When all kinds of trials and temptations crowd into your lives, my brothers, don't resent them as intruders, but welcome them as friends! Realize that they come to test your faith and to produce in you the quality of endurance. But let the process go on until that endurance is fully developed, and you will find you have become men of mature character with the right sort of independence. James 1:2-4

James says, "Welcome our troubles as friends!" Now let's be honest; that's a pretty idealistic and impractical comment. People who welcome troubles as friends are either self-styled martyrs or liars, aren't they? The truth of the matter is that we do resent our troubles as intruders — intruders on our dreams, intruders into our plans, intruders into our happiness. And it's usually better not to try to figure out the why or the wherefore of trouble, or you'll just wind up blaming God or feeling sorry for yourself. So don't give us that ivory-tower "welcome them as friends."

But James is serious. He wants us to know that right now — at this very time — there is a tremendous process going on in our personalities, one which has terrific implications for us. It's a process of restoration. Imagine a man finding his former friend in an isolated South Pacific island where he had been lost since World War II. The man is thin and sickly, scared and almost out of touch with life. The man brings his friend home and now begins to feed him carefully, to introduce him gradually to his former way of life. He was freed from his island "slavery" when the friend found him. But now comes the task of taking full advantage of that freedom, of reconstructing his personality around it again.

As a sinner, I am a slave to isolation, loneliness, and hopelessness. But God in Jesus Christ broke me free from that slavery. He shared my human existence that through

His death "He might destroy him who has the power of death . . . and deliver all those who through fear of death were subject to lifelong bondage."

But to be delivered doesn't mean to be fully living with that freedom. Since we have a nature so tied up with bondage to sin, to shortsightedness, to life without God, it's no simple matter suddenly to be God's free child. So God, who broke us free in the first place, now carries out a program of restoration aimed at developing our personalities and lives around that freedom. The heart of the program: to restore Himself to the center of our lives. As we try to push other things into the center — ambitions or pet sins, God has to keep shoving them out and Himself in.

This is where trouble is valuable! As our Father works at restoring balance to our life, balance centered in Him, He is determined to use both the good and the bad of life to do it. Obviously He did not create evil, nor does He will that things be bad. The sad story of where evil comes from is the sad story of rebellion and sin in us and our world. But granted that it is here, our heavenly Father insists on using it.

Each trouble keeps bringing up the issue of where God is in our lives. Are we getting along all right without Him? Is having Him and His life any part of our goals? Can we trust Him? Does He have to fulfill certain requirements before we will be happy with Him? The relation between our Father and us is both tested and clarified as we go through trouble together. Trouble produces in us the "quality of endurance." It's like an athlete in training, learning to give up things, learning to decide clearly what his goal is. Only our training is in letting God be God in our lives and letting Him have central place. God uses trouble to keep reshaping us into His image.

And if God can use good and bad that way, why can't we? Trouble can indeed come to all of us, but the results of that trouble are still in our hands. We can give up, resign ourselves to fate, or we can continue to look for and follow God's will, welcoming trouble as a part of the training.

So let's talk about troubles in our family:

Does being free in Christ show in my personality?

What goals might my Father still be trying to fulfill in me?

Do my goals and my Father's probably agree?

Which was the last serious trouble this family experienced?

How can we be different the next time we face trouble together?

You might want to close with this prayer:

Our Father in heaven, we confess that we often chafe and complain when we are troubled. Yet we thank You that in Christ Jesus You are restoring and changing us. Bend our wills that we may have room for You at all times, and move us to accept whatever means You choose.

Decisions

And if in the process any of you does not know how to meet any particular problem, he has only to ask God — who gives generously to all men without making them feel foolish or guilty — and he may be quite sure that the necessary wisdom will be given him. James 1:5

How much of our life depends on the decisions we make? We make a decision, and then we must live with it. And how often we realize only in retrospect how important the decision was! We decide what our lifework will be, we decide whom we will marry, we decide where we will live. All the decisions put together make the pattern of our lives.

Wouldn't it be interesting to stand off and look at the kind of pattern which is developing? Is it beautiful and meaningful, or is it a distorted hodge-podge?

Now there are several problems in making decisions. One of these is shortsightedness. We take the action which fits the moment best without considering future results. So a fellow may decide to go with a girl just because she's good looking and not care that she has a selfish personality. Or Dad can take a new job just because of the pay without considering the effect on his family and personal life. Sometimes we're shortsighted simply because we can't know everything, and at other times because we insist on being that way.

For God's people the problem of shortsightedness is even more significant. It is shortsightedness for one to make decisions without taking "the plan" into consideration. Other people may have no definite plan of life, but there is one for us. It's a pattern developed around the death and resurrection of Jesus Christ. The heart of the plan is that we not simply eke out 70 years on this planet in a more or less helter-skelter fashion. The plan of God is to give us life — the real thing — full of meaning and leading right up to God Himself. Now this plan began to move when Jesus died to free us from sin and rose to begin sharing with us His life. It would be a shame if we made and wove our plans with no regard for this really significant one!

This is where asking God comes in. First we agree that His is the master plan which we would like to accept for our lives. Isn't this the meaning of our Christian faith, that we accept Jesus as Lord? Then we will certainly grant that He should keep us going in the right direction. We're somewhat like the quarterback and the football coach. The quarterback calls the specific plays, but he is constantly checking with the coach because the coach is planning the game.

So we come to the "particular problems" which James is talking about: the right girl, the right job, the right house, the right neighborhood, the right kind of stand to take. We don't decide these simply on the basis of momentary feelings or even shortsighted goals. We want our heavenly Father to be right there in the center of all we do, keeping us full of wisdom — the wisdom which is His plan working out in our lives. So we pray with each decision, we ask for Him to show us His will.

Let's talk about the decisions we make:

> Why do I sometimes resist praying about a decision?
>
> Are there any decisions which ought to be "family ones"?
>
> How does God answer my prayer for wisdom?
>
> How do parents and teen-agers fit in when making decisions?
>
> Have I decided what to do with my life? Has this come under God's plan?

Here's a suggestion for your closing prayer:

Heavenly Father, we confess that we often run helter-skelter through life with little concern for Your plan. Open our hearts by Your power, and let us come to You frequently through Jesus Christ our Lord.

Doubts

But he must ask in sincere faith without secret doubts as to whether he really wants God's help or not. The man who trusts God, but with inward reservations, is like a wave of the sea, carried forward by the wind one moment and driven back the next. James 1:6

What's a big problem in prayer? Our doubts. They come in many shapes and sizes: Does prayer really help? Is God here with me now? And finally (we are almost embarrassed to admit it): Is there really a God? It's odd, when we want to be most confident, we find ourselves most shaky. Prayer is a real test of faith! It's so hard to pray without doubting.

There's more to make us uncomfortable. The Bible seems to leave no room for doubting. "Believe Me, if you have faith . . ." are the haunting words of Jesus on the subject of prayer. And how we wish that "if" weren't there! Now along comes James with "he must ask in sincere faith without secret doubts." So we often find ourselves feeling not only uncomfortable when we pray but also guilty — guilty because we have doubts when apparently we shouldn't. We feel like a wave of the sea all right, carried forward almost up to God's throne one moment and driven back full of doubt and guilt the next.

But aren't these doubts really pointing to a deeper problem? Aren't they really an indication of how "little" we let God be in our lives? This "littleness" shows up everywhere. We see little of His relation to the whole universe and His power over it. His will and plan for men occupies such a little place in our thinking. Worst of all He is *little more* than "God" — a high being, cold, distant; He is not our heavenly Father, loving, close, and real. What earthbound creatures we are, looking at God only through narrow, careful glances instead of letting Him shine forth in all His fullness and glory to us! So when it comes time to depend on Him, it's no wonder we doubt.

It's this littleness, though, that Christ changes. He appeared on earth to free us from being so guarded and doubtful with God. One of the really beautiful results of His work is that we begin to know what our heavenly Father is like. Christ came bringing life, and the life consisted in enjoying the fullness of God. It began to be apparent in the people whom He changed. Sinners came to Him for forgiveness; sick came for healing; beggars for help; discouraged for comfort. They saw something in Christ: the dawn of a new era for themselves. They saw that God was their Father in Christ, and they were suddenly starting to enjoy the situation.

Don't think they didn't come with doubts about themselves and their conditions. They must have been full of concerns and anxieties, but one thing they weren't doubting: that Jesus held the key, that their sole hope was tied up with Him. They had a heavenly Father; they knew that through Jesus. So they came.

When we pray, we don't pray without our mixed up emotions and feelings, it is true. But when we pray, there's no doubt about one thing — through Christ we have a heavenly Father, and He is full of love and power and understanding. So we have to ask ourselves, How well do we let God be great in our lives?

Let's think about this for a moment:

Can we see how we keep "reducing" God in our lives?
Do we reduce salvation to something after death?
Do our prayers reflect the fullness and greatness of God?
Is it easy to pray?
Is it true that older people have fewer doubts about God than teen-agers?

Would you like to close with this prayer?

Our heavenly Father, You know how many problems lurk in our hearts and minds when we come to pray. We thank You that through Jesus Christ we are Your beloved children and are invited to bring You all our cares. Give us, then, the faith to come to You at all times in His name.

13

Double-minded

That sort of man cannot hope to receive anything from God, and the life of a man of divided loyalty will reveal instability at every turn. James 1:7, 8

All kinds of people come to a basketball game. When we look over the crowd, it's obvious some get more out of it than others. The players get the most out of it because they're playing — they've really made up their minds to win! Then come the fans — they, too, know which team must win, so they have a terrific time. But we always feel sorry for the people who have been dragged along by a fan or just happened to drop in to see a game, any game. They never really get anywhere, because they can't make up their minds which side to join. They just cheer as best they can when a basket is made or smile at a close one, and generally try to be excited.

James gets impatient with people who can't make up their mind about being loyal to Christ. Could he mean me? As I look into my heart, do I find it irretrievably committed to following Christ or not?

Our Lord Christ did make life a challenge, didn't He? He entered it not as a disinterested spectator but as leader of a team that's bent on winning. "Fear not," He said, "you will receive the Kingdom." He made this kind of challenge out of life because He wasn't content to let us simply spring up at birth, flame up in middle age, and then fizzle out at death. Why should men be content with existence when the Father had created them for life — real life, eternal life, complete life? So He took up the challenge of gaining it for men and stayed with the battle right up to the cross, because He knew victory was His.

But granted His victory, He throws the challenge to us. Will we or will we not be His? He keeps driving at it. There are two roads in life — which one will we take? There are two goals in life — which one is ours? There are two masters — which will we serve? So we could define our Christian faith as a matter of loyalty. Will we be loyal to Christ, the Leader of our salvation, or not?

This loyalty is no pushover though. Life without Him has too many aspects that are attractive. For one thing, we were born with a natural inclination to ignore Him. It can be so natural and easy to forget, to disobey, to turn away. For another, loyalty to Christ means a cost. It is the cost of acceptance by Christ instead of acceptance by our crowd. The cost involves struggling with pet sins instead of giving in to them; it takes the form of living by faith instead of by sight. We like the idea of being loyal to Christ, but it does have problems.

Thank God, He has not let us struggle through this problem alone. Christ, who throws out the challenge to follow Him, sends His Holy Spirit to people just to make it possible. The Holy Spirit is the "new mind" in them pulling and tugging for the life of loyalty. But that leaves us with two minds: the Holy Spirit urges us to be loyal to Christ; our natural inclinations look at the other possibilities.

So there's our issue. It's not really one of will power or insight as we see Christ. It's rather one of listening to the Holy Spirit within us. He is there, and He is active. But to what extent do we obey His prompting?

This is something to discuss:

> How would my life be different if I were completely loyal to Christ?
>
> Can I use my baptism in this struggle?
>
> What is my greatest problem in being loyal to Christ?
>
> What will I do about it tomorrow?

Here's a prayer suggestion:

Lord Jesus Christ, we thank You for entering the world to bring life to us and are happy that You won the victory. We confess that many times we still look to other things and compromise our loyalty to You. Send us Your Holy Spirit in all His power to make us able to be loyal all our lives to Your exciting challenge.

Money

The brother who is poor may be glad because God has called him to the true riches. The rich may be glad that God has shown him his spiritual poverty. For the rich man, as such, will wither away as surely as summer flowers. One day the sunrise brings a scorching wind; the grass withers at once and so do all the flowers — all that lovely sight is destroyed. Just as surely will the rich man and all his extravagant ways fall into the blight of decay. James 1:9-11

Money is certainly a topic for the family to discuss. Whose is it? How much does a teen-ager deserve? How shall we divide it? Plenty of family arguments start over money. Do teen-agers and parents have a working understanding about money in this family?

James assumes that his readers will include rich and poor. After all, becoming a Christian will not necessarily make us lose everything, nor will it guarantee success in every venture. So down through the ages there have been rich and poor Christians. But James also assumes that both rich and poor Christians have discovered something about money. What's more, he assumes they have both discovered the same thing about it, and this assumption leads him to say they can both rejoice though one may have plenty and the other may be destitute.

Their discovery? That money is quite fragile. It is a very weak and undependable thing, very much tied to the present and able to be rendered completely worthless. On the surface this can sound like ivory-tower philosophy. We all pay a certain lip service to this kind of thinking, but no one really expects to light a hundred-dollar bill and watch it burn. We don't expect it to fade that completely. Nor do we need to as long as — the country is financially sound, the government holds up, etc., etc.

But the discovery is more than an understanding of economics. The person who can use money without selling his soul to it has discovered something about life itself. He has discovered that many, many things in life are to be enjoyed only for the moment. Cut a beautiful flower, take it into the house, and enjoy it in all its beauty, for tomorrow it will be wilted and gone. Don't cry over its passing. Don't adore it as anything more than it is — a pretty flower. Our life is full of all kinds of beautiful things, but they are cut flowers — beautiful for the moment and no more. Wonderful to enjoy but *not to live for.*

The treasures of life lie elsewhere: in living for a purpose, in having a goal which cannot be destroyed, in being able to love and be loved. The true riches are those permanent features of life which not even the grave can take away from us. They are available to us, not by way of the bank but by way of the cross, where our Lord Jesus Christ, "though He was rich, yet for your sakes . . . became poor that ye through His poverty might be rich."

So both the rich and the poor know about life. The poor man does not need to curse God because he has no money. He's been deprived of some attractive possibilities, it's true, but not of life. The rich man rejoices tremendously that he didn't fall into the trap of thinking he had everything — a kind of reasoning that would have deprived him of the treasure of the cross.

How we use our money reveals our view of life. We can sell ourselves out to things, or we can be engaged in the pursuit of the true riches.

So let's talk:

Does this family have a pretty good understanding of money?

Does the way we spend it betray any selling out to "things"?

Can a Christian be ambitious about making money?

How much do we give to God?

Here's a prayer suggestion:

Our heavenly Father, thank You for providing the needs and wants of our bodies and giving us so many things to enjoy. Help us to use all these gifts for what they are and never to get lost in them to the exclusion of our rich treasury of eternal life through Jesus Christ, our Lord.

Temptations

The man who patiently endures the temptations and trials that come to him is the truly happy man. For once his testing is complete, he will receive the crown of life which the Lord has promised to all who love Him. A man must not say when he is tempted, "God is tempting me." For God has no dealings with evil and does not Himself tempt anyone. No, a man's temptation is due to the pull of his own inward desires, which can be enormously attractive. His own desire takes hold of him, and that produces sin. And sin in the long run means death — make no mistake about that, brothers of mine. James 1:12-15

Temptation may not be easy for us to talk about. No one likes to admit what his particular sins *really* are. Nor does a person quickly face temptation and get rid of it. It almost seems that our temptations are the spice of our lives; they let our secret selves do a little roaming from the straight and narrow. Who hasn't wondered what he would do if he were in a place where absolutely no one would know, no one would find out?

There's something mysterious about our temptations. We feel the tug of a force that defies description, and the very presence of that "pull" excites and mystifies us. We know it's wrong, we don't approve, yet — just this once — maybe for a moment —. What makes us do it? Why can't we decide to break the pattern and live above it? It looks so obvious on paper, in a Bible discussion, or when we are among others; but why do things change so quickly when the temptation comes?

James wants us to know that there's no real mystery about temptation at all. What temptation is, where it comes from, and where it leads are very plain.

Temptation is a pull, a tug on our personality. To call it a "pull" is to put it above the level of a mistake or a lack of information or even a lack of will power. There is tugging at the heart and core of each one of us, a pull which leads us into our decisions.

Or we could call the pull our inward desires. Originally God created man to desire actions which would please God, help his neighbor, and lead to God's glory. The "image of God" meant above all that God lived right in the desires of man. This no longer happens. Sin's fullest dimension appears in this, that our personality is formed not around God but around self-centered desires, a deliberate pull away from Him. James wants us to get an honest view of ourselves. The natural pull in a person is away from God. And in us, the restored people of God, that natural pull is still present. Though the Spirit now lives in us, pulling to God, our "nature" still tugs in the opposite direction.

In a situation, then, the tug comes right from within

ourselves. We have the basic equipment for forgetting God, and it becomes operative. And where do these tugs lead? To death. To become the slaves of temptation is to become slaves of death. For temptation leads to sin, and sin leads to eternal death. Temptations can be the strings by which Satan himself pulls us to his home in hell. But Satan doesn't have to be granted that kind of power. Powerful as our inward desires may be, they don't have to become the tools of Satan. We can say this because the Lord Jesus Christ has broken the power of Satan over our inward desires. When he faced Satan and conquered him, it was like tying up a mad dog. The dog can still kill someone, but only if the person insists on getting too close to him. Satan still roams the world, and he can still kill, but only with our consent. If we insist on being in places which abound in temptation, we can expect troubles. If we will do nothing to change deathly habits, we can hurt our souls. But only "if."

The situation has been decided once for all in Jesus Christ, and we are asked to be patient, resisting temptations down through our lives. We can excuse ourselves by claiming that God let us down, that the temptation was too much, but we're only kidding ourselves. The truth is: "A man's temptation is due to. . . ."

So let's talk:

> Just think about the whole matter of temptation: the "pull," the way out, the plan of God.
>
> Are young people tempted more than others?
>
> Are we of any help to one another in temptation?
>
> Is our family able to draw on God in our temptations?

Prayer:

Dear heavenly Father, we know that we are tempted because we desire much that is sinful. But we also know that Your Son has conquered the forces of evil and made it possible for us to break free from any temptation. Send us Your Holy Spirit to keep us firm in our faith that we may have the power to fight every temptation through the strength of Christ, our Lord.

Endowments

But every good endowment that we possess and every complete gift that we have received must come from above, from the Father of all lights, with whom there is never the slightest variation or shadow of inconsistency. By His own wish He made us His own sons through the Word of truth that we might be, so to speak, the first specimens of His new creation. James 1:16-18

Each of us has his set of basic endowments. Our brains, our voices, the background and environment in which we grow up are finally just "given" to us. There just isn't such a thing as a self-made man. Could the All-American quarterback have become that if he had been born without legs? Could the opera star have reached the top without the right vocal cords in the first place? Each of us has some outstanding, some mediocre, and some weak abilities, and we can't really take credit for having these.

But we can talk about what we will do with our endowments. The same set of brains can build a heart machine or destroy a city. A well-coordinated body can belong to a fair and healthy athlete or a conceited and mean one. We can even take a large inheritance of money and become wasteful or beneficial to society. And of course we certainly have plenty of examples for both. Sin shows itself in the way talents are misused in school, neighborhood, or anywhere else. So we spend a lot of time trying to get ourselves to use endowments responsibly. Our heavenly Father must be very interested in the results. After all, He gave the abilities. And finding His purpose for the abilities is the key to a meaningful life.

But for a Christian there's an added responsibility. We represent a double effort on God's part. Not only did He endow us with our abilities, He has made us His own sons. Everyone is God's child by creation, but we who have been reached through Jesus Christ are His "reclaimed" sons enjoying the full privileges and rights of such status. "By His own wish He made us His own sons through the Word of truth."

And what responsibility goes with the status? We are, "so to speak, the first specimens of His new creation." Imagine, we are the models of what God can do for a person. God wants every person to know that He can salvage him from a meaningless life, devoted to nothing in particular. He can make new persons. And as evidence He shows what He has done in us! We are the first ones off His assembly line, "the first specimens of His new creation."

What a responsibility! What a special responsibility for us! Belonging to Christ doesn't increase our abilities; it enables us to use them to the glory of God. Imagine the Christian beauty queen who leads a pure and God-fearing life. What an opportunity she has to be a pacesetter among her friends! What about the star outfielder who refuses to curse? His endowment in athletics enables him to lead others to a better understanding of life under God. And so it goes down the line. We can use our abilities to set the pace for the people around us, the pace of living to the glory of God.

So we need to talk about this:

What are the special endowments in this family?
How can they be pacesetting to people around us?
Do they lead us to self-glory and conceit?
Read Romans 12:1, 2 and talk about our being "living sacrifices" offering up our bodies to God.

Let's pray:

Thank You, dear Father, for the endowments of our lives. Thank You especially for giving us Your Holy Spirit to make us able to use them to Your glory. Accept the lives we offer up to You through Jesus Christ, our Lord.

Temper Control

In view of what He has made us, then, dear brothers, let every man be quick to listen but slow to use his tongue and slow to lose his temper. For man's temper is never the means of achieving God's true goodness. James 1:19, 20

The word "temper" might well be defined as "personality control." In our houses we usually have a heating apparatus of some sort and in one of the rooms a little device called the thermostat. The sum total of fuel energy, electrical power, and whatever else might make up our heating system is regulated by this little instrument.

In a human personality, too, there are all kinds of energies working. Our glands, our muscles, our thoughts, everything about us must work in some sort of harmony if we are to be any kind of person. Keeping our temper is really just keeping all of these in control. There's a positive side to discussing temper — the great value which comes from being able to harness all our energies to reach our goals.

There's a positive value for God too. He gives us our endowments to use in setting the pace of the world for Him. He has set us up as His children in Christ to be His stewards on earth. He has even come into our very personalities by His Holy Spirit to make Himself influential and forceful. He feeds us with His Word and sacrament to keep the Spirit living under His inner persuasion, devoting body, mind, and gifts to Him.

So why do we lose our temper? Isn't it really the indication of a struggle which continues to go on in our hearts? Our God, who reached down in Christ to save us, has to reach into every aspect of our personality to change us. Making us over from rebels to children is not a matter of signing a document but of changing a personality. So we know that within our hearts are all kinds of emotions, attitudes, strengths, and weaknesses. God's Spirit must conquer each one of these. We lose our tempers — some of us more easily than others — only because His Spirit is momentarily pushed aside and we give place to an emotion of rebellion.

The main point, however, is this: "Man's temper is never the means of achieving God's true goodness." Temper must be battled in us. It cannot achieve God's goodness, because it puts us above God. When we lose our temper, we usually talk when we should be listening, demand when we should be submitting. To lose our temper is to let nothing but our emotions count. The will of God and the concerns of others are shoved aside.

So here's a place to talk about self-crucifixion. When Jesus told us to take up our cross and follow Him, He wasn't only making a demand for us to meet — but also describing a new situation. The person who has come to the cross of Christ has received a new ability, the ability to crucify those features of his own personality which don't belong there. Jesus expects much of His disciples, but that expectation underscores the really thrilling change He has brought.

So we can talk about controlling tempers. We who are Christ's can set up a cross and on it hang our tendency to lose our temper. The cross is actually our determination filled with Christ's power. What could be more challenging than to follow Christ in such a way?

So let's talk about this:

How would I be different if I took this passage seriously?

What difference would it make for our family?
How can we help one another in this?

A prayer suggestion:

Our Father in heaven, forgive us for so frequently losing our tempers and thereby hindering Your work. Help us change any habits or attitudes which You desire changed, in Christ, our Lord.

Personal Morals

Have done, then, with impurity and every other evil which touches the lives of others, and humbly accept the message that God has sown in your hearts and which can save your souls.
James 2:21

Mention "church" or Christianity, and many people think of restrictions, a whole set of rules to keep us from having fun. Some teen-agers seem to think that all that parents want to do is make rules, and some parents think that all that teen-agers want to do is break them! So when we sit down as a family to talk about personal morals, there can very well be a large gap which will have to be bridged.

So let's do it this way: Let's start with God. Did He dream up a set of rules to cramp our style and set us apart from others? Is He so far out of touch with life that He can't know or care how much we miss by having to obey Him? We can hardly say this. In fact, as we begin to look into our Scriptures, we find that our Father didn't start men out with a code of conduct at all. He could do this because He created men with a complete love for Him and for each other. Instead of rules He gave love. There were no rules, because they were unnecessary.

But think of the force which made rules unnecessary: a complete love for God and each other. With this kind of love no one would ever hurt any other person. And think also of how far we are from that happy condition. We certainly see sin in our readiness to hurt one another and ourselves. Absent from our lives is the urge to live with and for others to our happiness and God's glory.

So the rules become necessary. With heavy heart God has to spell out practical restrictions and guides. Sex can become so completely selfish and hurtful that He has to put restrictions on our relations with one another. Our tongue can do so terribly much damage that God has to spell out the right way to use it. In fact, each of our desires can lead to the hurt of others instead of their health, and therefore there must be a definition of right and wrong.

But we're Christ's people, and this means we don't just have a code of ethics to use. Christ's coming to earth has a direct influence on our relationship to others. He was busy restoring our relation to God by His suffering and dying, and the result is that through faith God begins to live in us. The Holy Spirit is God living in us directly and powerfully. He is sent to us by Christ and is basic to our Christian personality. So if God lives in us, we are able to love people instead of hurting them. Then there will be in us that force which makes us direct our actions to the health of people instead of their hurt.

Or to put it in the practical words of James, when the message of God is sown in our hearts, our souls begin to take a new turn. That message is not just a piece of information for our minds, but the powerful means by which the Holy Spirit gets into our personality and changes it.

So, for us, personal morals have a whole new twist. They aren't restrictions on good times. They are restrictions only on our old sinful tendencies and, what's more important, they show us how to practice love to others. Love is worked out in personal attitudes and habits.

A person's morals are Christian when for Christ's sake he is living to God and others, not just himself.

So let's talk:

> Do my standards come from my relation to God?
>
> Do all of us agree on what's right and wrong in this family?
>
> How can we make God the important One in personal morals?

Here's a prayer suggestion:

Our Father, we thank You for creating us to live with one another. Forgive us for so often forgetting other people. Fill us with Your Spirit so that we may love all others and live in peace with them, through Christ, our Lord.

How to Read Scripture

Don't, I beg of you, only hear the message, but put it into practice; otherwise you are merely deluding yourselves. The man who simply hears and does nothing about it is like a man catching the reflection of his own face in a mirror. He sees himself, it is true, but he goes on with whatever he was doing without the slightest recollection of what sort of person he saw in the mirror. But the man who looks into the perfect mirror of God's Law, the Law of liberty, and makes a habit of so doing, is not the man who sees and forgets. He puts that Law into practice, and he wins true happiness. James 1:22-25

What's the real problem in reading Scripture? Words too hard? Can't find a good time? Can't seem to get interested? We usually haggle around with these kinds of problems. How about looking into ourselves?

Let's imagine a girl looking into her mirror in the morning at a head of unruly hair. She doesn't expect anyone important to come around, so she doesn't bother to comb it. Before long her latest crush comes by, and she's happily talking with him. It isn't until after he's gone that she glances into the mirror again and realizes what a mess she was. Horrors! She had given the mirror only a perfunctory glance in the morning and so had completely forgotten. Take the same girl, same mirror, but getting ready for a date, and see the difference. This time she's looking for what needs to be changed because she wants to look her very best.

That's why James compares the Word to a mirror. It can be of value to us only if we approach it to look for changes that need to be made with regard to our estimate of ourselves, our conduct, our relation to God.

The trouble with looking into our Scripture mirror is that the conditions needing change are more than mere messy hair. Our relation to God is constantly being affected by the wear and tear of life. Sins crop up and thrive, our faith sputters and cools. The Word keeps showing us these problems and showing the way through them. But the way isn't always easy. When the Word is telling us to abandon a sin, we'd rather walk away with only a mental understanding of what the words say, not with an attempt to put them into practice. Even when it's pointing straight to Christ, we don't easily give ourselves to simply believing.

So it's often "safer" not to take the Word seriously. We spend a lot of time getting the meaning of the words of a Bible passage, arguing about general implications, debating various propositions, but that's all. This is easier than asking, "How would I be different if I took this seriously?" or, "How would my family be different if I took this seriously?" or, "What difference would it make for my friends if I took this seriously?"

Yet that's what the law of liberty is all about. God has not given us a dead book of propositions which can be memorized, and that's all. He is expressing Himself to us through His Word, and His relation to us hinges on it.

Our Father moves toward us through the message contained in those pages. As He does, there are sure to be results. The openness of our hearts is rewarded with the presence of His Spirit. As He graciously leads us to faith, He also gently pushes us out into life. Our contact with the Scriptures has been an interchange with the Holy Spirit. Not only do we see the direction our life must go — in Christ we have the ability to follow it.

"Put the message into practice" means: "Apply what you read. *Use* the power of the Spirit." Don't just read about it.

Let's talk about this:

How much do I try out what the Word says?

Do I avoid the message of Scripture?

Do I approach it ready to be changed?

Here's a prayer suggestion:

Our Father, we appreciate Your patience and mercy in dealing with us as Your children. We know that often we have no desire to do what You tell us. Grant us willing hearts and power to do what You tell us in the Word; through Jesus Christ, our Lord.

Our Tongues

If anyone appears to be "religious" but cannot control his tongue, he deceives himself, and we may be sure that his religion is useless. James 1:26

"Why did I say it?" How often we've wished the word hadn't slipped out of our mouths! We didn't really mean it, it wasn't really true, yet there we were blurting it out like silly fools. It makes us wonder why we *do* say the things we do.

Some people use their tongues to make an impression. For some reason or other they don't feel quite big enough in their group, so they try to look bigger than they really are. They tell those juicy stories or use those shocking words or spread that tempting gossip because then people listen and they feel as if they occupy space for a little while anyway. Is that my reason?

Others deliberately want to hurt someone. They hate someone and don't miss a chance to tear him down. We can fight a real battle with someone and win a great victory just by the things we say. Is that why I said it?

Or we can use our tongues to let off steam. We've had our feelings hurt, or we didn't get our way, or something didn't go right, and now we're angry. It just pours out. We've got to get back at somebody somehow. So we say something mean, or we curse, or we make someone else unhappy. True, we don't feel much better as a result, but that was the reason we did it. Could this be true of me?

A pretty volatile little instrument is that tongue of ours. We can do a lot of bad with it.

But must it be that way? Is that just the way we are, and nothing can be done about it? God certainly didn't create our tongues for making false impressions or deliberately hurting or letting off steam. What does He want from them? He has some wonderful uses for our words.

He gave us our tongues to declare His glory. Can a tree write a poem? Can a dog speak a psalm? Can an animal explain the intricacies of an atom? Our tongues can be useful in expressing the glory of God.

He gave us our tongues to cement our fellowship. When people quit talking with one another, we know they aren't getting along. It's just basic to human relations that we talk to one another. Our words can make love grow and can strengthen friendships. We need our words to live with one another.

And because many of God's children are still wandering around oblivious to Him, God uses our tongues to bring them back. How else can we find out the way of salvation in Jesus our Lord but through the words of God's people?

So the tongue has all kinds of possibilities for good or evil. The difference lies in our religion. We are new people in Christ. As such every part of our personality has been reached and changed by His work. He died to forgive our terrible sins of the tongue and rose to make our tongues beautiful instruments of God again. He not only saves us from a sad fate at the end of our life, but right now He turns us from worthless habits to living worship. So we're able to face the questions: Is religion for us the willing worship of God seven days a week, or is it completely unrelated to life? Are we actually living in the newness of Christ? Our tongues are a good test.

So let's talk:

What does "religion" mean to me?

How would I change if my tongue were always worshiping God?

What specific resolution can I make about my tongue?

Prayer:

Our Father in heaven, we thank You for our tongues. Forgive us for all the abuses to which we have put them, and help us by the power of Your Spirit to use the new opportunities which have been given to our tongues by our Lord Christ.

Genuine Religion

Religion that is pure and genuine in the sight of God the Father will show itself by such things as visiting orphans and widows in their distress and keeping oneself uncontaminated by the world. James 1:27

Not all religion is genuine. Much of it is either an attempt to impress people or a sort of personal selfishness aimed at being saved while others are lost.

The Bible is full of shots at "false religion." People who say "Lord, Lord," but whose heart is far from Christ; Pharisees who stole widows' houses and for a pretense made long prayers; and brothers who talk about love but turn down a brother's need for food — all come in for severe criticism in its pages. So it makes us ask ourselves, What about us is not genuine? How could our "religion" be purer? We can look at several areas and talk about each.

It's not genuine when there is a tremendous gap between Sunday and Monday. Ours is always the temptation to keep what happens in church general and unrelated to our lives. To sing fervently, pray eloquently, and listen intently is a beautiful exercise. But our Lord tells us that unless our lives are devoted to Him, He cannot accept the Sunday morning offer.

It's not genuine when there is an absence of serving love. Our Lord Christ put us into a tremendous debt to all men. He knows we can't do anything for Him to pay back His love to us. So He has told us to do it to "the humblest of My brothers." We just can't be living our religion unless we are devoted to serving others. How does our family come out on this one?

It's not genuine when there is no battle with sin. That there is sin in our hearts is fact; that there is opportunity for sin in our world is fact; and that we will therefore be tending to sin is but the sad conclusion. So there must be a battle with sin whether it exists as greed, jealousy, envy, or in any other form. If our religion never makes us uncomfortable, never leads to any problems, never poses choices, we must examine its genuineness. Is our family keeping itself "uncontaminated by the world"?

It's true, this side of the grave we won't reach perfection in practicing our religion. Those who think they can do so have fallen into either blind conceit or blind despair. But the balance in our attempts lies in our Lord Jesus Christ. He gives us the right motive for practicing our religion. We don't practice it to gain access to God. We practice it because we already belong to God.

We practice our religion as His disciples. He called men not simply to have Him or to use Him but to follow Him. What men were originally created for, He made possible again: a relation of worshiping God with our whole life.

So let's talk about it:

Do I worship God full time?

Do I practice *serving* love?

Am I trying to keep myself "uncontaminated by the world"?

Here's a prayer suggestion:

Lord Christ, we rejoice that You entered the world to call us as disciples. Give us genuine religion, devoted not to self-centered goodness but to living entirely for You.

Snobbery

Don't ever attempt, my brothers, to combine snobbery with faith in our glorious Lord Jesus Christ! Suppose one man comes into your meeting well dressed and with a gold ring on his finger, and another man, obviously poor, arrives in shabby clothes. If you pay special attention to the well-dressed man by saying, "Please sit here — it's an excellent seat," and say to the poor man, "You stand over there, please, or if you sit, sit on the floor," doesn't that prove that you are making class distinctions in your mind and setting yourselves up to assess a man's quality? — a very bad thing. For do notice, my brothers, that God chose poor men, whose only wealth was their faith, and made them heirs to the Kingdom promised to those who love Him. And if you behave as I have suggested, it is the poor man that you are insulting. Look around you. Isn't it the rich who are always trying to "boss" you? Isn't it the rich who drag you into litigation? Isn't it usually the rich who blaspheme the glorious name by which you are known? James 2:1-7

Let's think specifically about the members of our congregation. Aren't many of them easier to be with than others? What is our standard of judgment? Isn't it all too frequently their "status" in life? How many close friends do we have in our congregation who are not more or less of our "class" or "type"? And when someone we consider "below" us tries to become our friend, don't we often feel a sort of resentment? We focus on our congregation because James says, "Don't ever attempt to combine snobbery with faith," and because we can't very well live in our community what we can't make work in our church.

This kind of snobbery comes too easily, doesn't it? It's so easy to go by appearances. The sweet aura of success, the warm glow of popularity always make an impression. We so quickly go from appearances to a judgment about how much someone is worth. "Candid Camera" once had the same man ask for a cigarette from different people; each time he altered his appearance between that of a wealthy businessman and that of a rather ordinary "commoner." Guess when he got the cigarettes (often a whole pack) and when he wasn't given a second look! The poor, the uneducated, the unattractive have a way of being uncompelling. We find it easy to overlook them.

Furthermore, we are concerned about the kind of people

we let be close to us. We don't mind being kind to a person "below" us as long as others don't get the impression that we are equals. Our own status gets involved in the people we befriend, and there it is again — snobbery! We don't want to take the risk of losing status because of them. Right in our own congregation there are plenty of people we won't reach out for in other than a condescending "keep your place and be grateful" sort of way. We combine faith and snobbery. And this combination doesn't work God's righteousness.

For one thing we're often so horribly wrong when we judge people this way. James asks if it isn't often the "important people" who oppress and keep *you* in line. And how many times haven't we learned to our dismay of a very warm and wonderful trait in a person we had frankly tended to disregard. Fortunately God doesn't judge by appearances, and He wants us to know it. What a person is goes a lot deeper than what appears on the surface. How well do we really know those people whom we ignore? Do we give them any chance to be themselves, or do we prejudge them and confine them to a place beneath us without even a hearing?

There's a much sadder aspect to this snobbery, though, than just mistaking character. It denies the Gospel of Christ. Christ came into this world to save every lost child of God. He went to a great deal of trouble to make that possible, as witness His humble life on earth, His patient endurance before scoffers like Pilate, His painful agony on that splintery cross. How He must love every last person in this world to have done so much! And now He tenderly commits to us the task of reaching those people. And we make distinctions! We rush to the beautiful and insult the ugly. How we frustrate His desire that we all be one! How we deprive Him of the joy of His labors! The "Lord of Glory" certainly doesn't get to enjoy His glory when we narrow down His love in such a way.

So He has made it possible for us to love anyone! With His own glory He has exalted every lowly, unattractive, uncompelling person in our neighborhood. These are the ones whom He singles out to stand beside in our world and call His brothers. Can't get close to that person? Squint your eyes and look again. See Christ standing right beside Him, saying, "Why, this is My brother!"

So let's talk:

How would I be different in my congregation if I put this Bible reading into practice?

Whom can I reach out to soon?

Can I do it?

And let's pray:

We confess, Lord Jesus, that even among the people of our own congregation we are constantly making distinctions in our love. Forgive us our snobbery, and exalt our fellow members in our eyes that we may love them as we know You do.

Prejudice

If you obey the royal Law, expressed by the scripture, "Thou shalt love thy neighbor as thyself," all is well. But once you allow any invidious distinctions to creep in, you are sinning; you have broken God's Law. Remember that a man who keeps the whole Law but for a single exception is nonetheless a lawbreaker. The one who said, "Thou shalt not commit adultery," also said, "Thou shalt do no murder." If you were to keep clear of adultery but were to murder a man, you would have become a breaker of God's whole Law. James 2:8-11

Can we American Christians help seeing racial prejudice getting its proper condemnation in this passage? Isn't James's stern point about a "single exception" an introductory warning not to turn aside quickly from this issue as "blown out of proportion" or "not really essential" or with some such weak excuse? And can we fail to look for that prejudice right in our own hearts? No matter what our own particular color or geography, can we say it doesn't happen here? All the labeling of areas or wringing of philosophic hands will not cover the fact that *we* stand guilty of making an "invidious distinction," one based on the color of skin. Granted in another land at another time the passage might well imply something different, but how about us?

Put all the arguments and debates together — open housing, integrated schools, gangs, intermarriage — and we can come out with all sorts of pros and cons. But let all the truths, half-truths, and deliberate lies be what they may, isn't James calling for a different perspective? Isn't the first concern of my heavenly Father whether or not I *love* my neighbor, and isn't this the question He continues to ask as I try to throw up a tremendous smoke screen of problems, arguments, and heated words? Let the smoke settle, and He still wants to know, "Do you love him as well as you do yourself?"

So where are our problems of prejudice? For some of us it's a matter of being unwilling to love without reservation. Such love is possible only when we can feel completely comfortable with someone. The test of a strangeness in any form is too much for us to pass. Because of all the associations which have been built up on a particular hue, we feel strange, and the result is that we cannot love. How we need the fullness of God's way of loving to fill our hearts so that we can share just a little of it with people!

For others of us, the focus of our trouble may be on what we're unwilling to do. We are afraid to upset anything. We've grown so accustomed to being completely like the people we live with that we don't want to upset our relation with them. We've developed the habit of being accepted and of accepting them. So we must accept their attitudes. We feel the wrongness of what is being perpetrated on a segment of God's people, but we just don't have the courage to do anything about it. And if we live in an area which unfortunately doesn't force any concrete demands on us, we can keep on avoiding the issue. We need the conviction of the Holy Spirit to convince the world rather than accept it and its attitudes.

But for all of us the trouble is that we put our own desires above God's. He expresses Himself in His law, and we immediately say that we are going to obey. But what is the practical result? We make exceptions. What meets our approval we heartily endorse and do. But what we think demands too much or too great a change or seems undesirable to us — this we conveniently forget. That way we can keep on assuming our goodness. Because we don't kill, we feel righteous; small matter that we hate a little.

And so in the last analysis it is not God's will but ours which is supreme. We will consider racial concerns not from God's standpoint but ours. We will act not according to love but according to self-interest. What does this do to our prayer "Thy will be done"?

This kind of look at ourselves drives us to a rather common place for the Christian: the foot of the cross. How we need forgiveness as we see the ugly marks of prejudice, of resistance to God's will right within ourselves! And the foot of the cross is a good place to go, for the Savior not only gives that forgiveness, He also sends us back to our problems in a new way. He sends us back viewing every person as a child of God and ourselves as servants of God. The petty shortcomings of our personalities are caught up in the greater sweep of God's love to all men. We begin to have the mind of Christ.

Christ conquers prejudice because Christ conquers us!

Think about the contributions we have made to "peace" among men.

Can we talk about these now?

Our prayer:

Lord, forgive us for being so small-hearted and fearful; forgive us our refusal to face Your claims and let Your will be done. Show us the way we are to go, and set and keep us on it through Your Holy Spirit.

Freedom

Anyway, you should speak and act as men who will be judged by the law of freedom. The man who makes no allowances for others will find none made for him. It is still true that "mercy smiles in the face of judgment." James 2:12, 13

"Freedom" is an important concern of parents and teen-agers. We know that as we mature we gain our freedom and learn to make a responsible use of it. So families go through many hours discussing how late we can stay out, what kind of rules apply to parties in the house, and how much authority parents can have over the friends we pick. Every family has to hammer out a working set of understandings. But granted the rules, how does a Christian family best reflect the will of God in this matter called freedom?

The starting point for our family is to put ourselves under the law of freedom. This means that we have no intention of gaining access to God or getting into heaven by scrupulously following a code of goodness. We look at ourselves and see that no such goodness is attainable. The few things we do which conform to any righteous law are hardly adequate to change the deep and obvious sinfulness which we exhibit on every hand. We know good and well that our one hope to stand confidently before God is that in Christ He will forgive what we have done and "replace judgment with mercy." Each member of our family will stand before God with that mercy as his key to life.

But where do we go from there? Do we breathe a big sigh of relief and begin a life full of any old kind of sin we want? Hardly. "Can a person who has become one with Christ live in sin?" the apostle Paul asks. The essence of Christian liberty is our being one with Christ through faith in Him so that He lives in us. The goal is not that I arrive at what I can do and still not sin, but that Christ dwell in me in all my personality. Words like "maturing, growing, discipline" are related to *this* goal.

So teen-agers have parents, and parents have teen-agers. If I am a Christian parent I am certainly responsible for the development of my teen-ager. To let him go unguided into life is to be derelict in my duty as parent. But on the other hand I cannot adopt some rigid code which leaves no room for his freedom. If I make no allowances for his mistakes, have absolutely no concern for his problems, and make no provisions for his developing maturity, I have substituted a set of rules for the indwelling power of Christ. And in exalting some rule above all else I have probably forgotten that I will be given mercy because *God makes allowances for me*.

If I am a Christian teen-ager and make no allowances for my parents, I, too, am abusing my freedom. To give my parents no benefit of being more mature, to judge them simply by other parents, to despise them for any mistakes they may make is to overlook that Christ has been merciful to me and that I expect Him to be merciful when I stand before Him.

The essence of a Christian family is this shared freedom which comes from a mutual life in Christ. Rules made with no trust, codes established with no understanding leave little room for Christ to be the heart of obedience. On the other hand, rules broken with no concern, codes rejected with no responsibility overlook the very nature of that freedom. So here's a good place for us to talk together.

So let's talk about this:

How can we develop this kind of "freedom" in our family?

How would this make a difference in our family?

Prayer:

Thank you, heavenly Father, for reclaiming us as Your children in Jesus Christ. Help us follow Him in thought, word, and deed, so that our freedom will be to His glory.

Putting Faith into Practice

Now what use is it, my brothers, for a man to say he "has faith" if his actions do not correspond with it? Could that sort of faith save anyone's soul? If a fellow man or woman has no clothes to wear and nothing to eat and one of you say, "Good luck to you, I hope you'll keep warm and find enough to eat," and yet give them nothing to meet their physical needs, what on earth is the good of that? Yet that is exactly what a bare faith without a corresponding life is like — useless and dead. If we only "have faith," a man could easily challenge us by saying: "You say that you have faith and I have merely good actions. Well, all you can do is to show me a faith without corresponding actions, but I can show you by my actions that I have faith as well." James 2:14-17*

"Now what use is it . . . for a man to say he 'has faith' if his actions do not correspond with it?" We get an uncomfortable feeling when we think about actions corresponding to faith. Actually we would like to live by a fiction — the fiction that there is some sort of invisible wall dividing what we are inside from what shows outside. No one can look into another's heart, and aren't we glad for that! No one can look inside to see what I'm really like; he can only take what I show on the outside and surmise from that. And perhaps I'm a lot better than I look! In fact, this is exactly what I like to protest, that I'm really more inside than appears on the outside.

But this is fiction. How fictitious it is we begin to realize when we observe our Lord Christ at the last judgment using the lives of people to demonstrate what kind of faith they had. And as we go back through our New Testaments, we note that Jesus was always taking everyday examples from life to talk about faith and the results of faith.

But when I start to look at my life to see what kind of faith is there I get that uncomfortable feeling. How much faith, for example, shows up in my helpfulness to others? "Good luck to you, I hope you'll keep warm and find enough to eat." How many times haven't I let someone else's need bring no more than an expression of concern from me! "Good luck" I seem to keep saying over and over again to the needs of others, needs in which I could very well be helpful. It's usually not needs for food but the need of a person for a friend, the need of a friend for support, the need of a neighbor for loyalty which are my challenge. Good luck — is that all I ever seem to give people?

I even like to say "good luck" to Christ. How many times hasn't He been the One who needed me? There I was in the usual crowd, and Christ was looking for someone to set the pace. How He needed someone to turn our conversation to love instead of the way we were tearing someone down! And I wished I had the courage to turn the tide because I knew I could have done it. But I wished Christ "good luck" and kept my peace. There I was out with a friend. And how Christ needed someone to witness! But I wished Christ "good luck" and forgot about it.

Even in the setting of my church I often hope more for luck than anything else. Good luck to the choir, good luck to the Sunday school teachers, good luck to the young people's group! May they all succeed! But when have I let my faith speak out in my congregation as I saw opportunities of serving Christ through the simple means of our choir, our youth group, or our service groups?

Getting my actions to correspond to my faith is the challenge of my life. Thanks be to God, He has moved in to make this possible. When He made me His child in Baptism, He wasn't content to let me tuck my faith deep into my heart to keep it from being overexposed. For with that faith went the Holy Spirit deep into my heart. And once there, the Holy Spirit will not be denied. He lives in me and is striving to get control of me. That means I can do it! If I accept some of those opportunities, I will succeed, because that's all the Holy Spirit is waiting for. Bring on the opportunity. I can put my faith into practice.

So let's talk about this:

What are some of the opportunities to put my faith into practice?

How have I fared with these in the past?

Do I give the Holy Spirit a chance?

Prayer:

Holy Spirit, we thank You for living in our hearts to make our lives worthwhile. Take over the control of our minds that we may accept the opportunities of faith and have actions that correspond, for we ask in the name of Christ, our Lord.

Faith — Fact or Force

To the man who thinks that faith by itself is enough I feel inclined to say, "So you believe that there is one God? That's fine. So do all the devils in hell, and shudder in terror!" For, my dear shortsighted man, can't you see far enough to realize that faith without the right actions is dead and useless? Think of Abraham, our ancestor. Wasn't it his action which really justified him in God's sight when his faith led him to offer his son Isaac on the altar? Can't you see that his faith and his actions were, so to speak, partners — that his faith was implemented by his deed? That is what the Scripture means when it says:

And Abraham believed God,
And it was reckoned unto him for righteousness;
And he was called the friend of God.

A man is justified before God by what he does as well as by what he believes. Rahab, who was a prostitute and a foreigner, has been quoted as an example of faith, yet surely it was her action that pleased God when she welcomed Joshua's reconnoitering party and got them safely back by a different route. Yes, faith without action is as dead as a body without a soul.
James 2:18-26

Several things must be said about this passage before we take up its challenge. The first is that James is talking specifically to us as believers, not to unbelievers. He is accepting the cry of those who claim to have faith and are maintaining that they don't have to have any life of response, because "faith is enough." For another, the issue is not whether Christ is the only means of salvation or not. James presupposes this all the way through. He knows well enough that it is Christ who gains salvation for us, not our works. The issue is this: Can a man narrow down the meaning of the word "faith" to merely knowing that Christ died and expect to be saved by that? Can faith be just a fact in our life, or must it be a force?

It's a fact in our life when all we do is learn it, memorize it, repeat it. We can describe exactly what happened on

Good Friday and can rehearse the story of His birth. Faith becomes a body of knowledge to be mastered, and we have done that. Just as we learn world history or mathematics, so we have learned Christianity, and we call that faith. To such a view James gives the horrible information: The devils have that kind of faith!

Faith is a force when there's something going on inside us, when there's something alive in us. Better yet: when *Someone* is alive in us, for that's what really happens in faith. Faith is seeing the Lord Christ as the Hope of my life and enfolding Him into my heart. I am putting all my trust in Him, and I want Him as part of my life more than anything else. And He has told us how we can have Him: "Take up your cross and follow Me." So the result is to be one of His followers, to take up the life which He has offered. If faith is a trust in Christ as complete Savior and living Lord, the emphasis is on *Him* — the living One — not on a set of teachings by themselves. All the doctrines are so necessary just because they leave us standing beside *Him*. And once we have made the journey to His side, we are going to be plunged into a life of discipleship. There just isn't any other kind of faith.

So I must ask myself, Is Christ alive in me? We can assume that I have been taught and will continue to learn. But what is happening while this teaching takes place? Is Christ taking a firm grip on me and leading me into challenges and situations which will use me as His follower? Is He becoming a vital part of me? Or am I content to learn about Him instead of getting to know Him better?

Unfortunately I do try to content myself with knowledge instead of discipleship. I do this because it makes a convenient way to avoid the issues of my life. If Christ is taking over my life, this creates problems; problems when I don't want to give up certain habits, problems when I see a clear desire of His and don't want to fulfill it. So I tuck

Christ back into the information part of my mind. That way He and my life can go along side by side without influencing one another.

But Christ describes discipleship in living terms. He talks about continuing in His Word, obeying His commandments, loving Him. So we're left with James's question to discuss now. Is faith a fact for me — or a force?

Let's talk about it:

Is my faith a matter of knowledge — or of discipleship?
Would there be more challenges if my faith were more alive?
Can I think of instances?

Let's pray:

Lord Jesus Christ, remind us that You are calling us to be Your followers today. Forgive our attempts to put You back into history as a long-ago fact, and come into us through Your Holy Spirit that we may be live and active witnesses to the faith which is in us.

Teachers

Don't aim at adding to the number of teachers, my brothers, I beg you! Remember that we who are teachers will be judged by a much higher standard. James 3:1

Actually James isn't issuing a general discouragement to the teaching profession. He's getting at a rather basic aspect of our lives: the desire to set ourselves up as another person's teacher. How often don't we know what's right for someone else and promptly set out to show him! By getting at this issue James gives us fruitful ground for discussing this whole business of being another's teacher and of our relations to one another. We can think of teacher-student, pastor-people, parent-teen-ager, and many others. What really goes on here? The implications fit just as nicely into being taught as into teaching.

There are some serious implications to being a teacher. As soon as I elect to teach another, I am putting myself into a more searching position. Every teacher is finally setting up standards by which he first of all will be judged. Can a teacher denounce laziness and then waste his time? Can a pastor extol the merits of Bible reading and then fail to read it himself? Can a parent condemn waste and then throw his money away? How can I teach someone else to love his neighbor and not be condemning any hatred which exists in me? As soon as one of us begins to teach another, we set ourselves up for being taken at our word. By that teaching we will be judged by men, by the people we teach, by God.

So before we teach anyone, we had better ask why. And we had better ask why before we refuse to be taught. After all, our refusal is a sign we want to be teacher instead of learner. Frequently it's because we want to be superior to others. We can establish a certain position by it. Do we ever make it difficult for teachers at high school just because we don't like the idea of letting them be our superiors? Do we ever put down the teen-ager in our family just because we are griped that he doesn't recognize our superiority? Who is greatest is a big question that keeps popping up in our minds, and we like to answer it with teaching.

But our Lord Christ took the opposite approach. Taking a basin of water and a towel, He began to wash the feet of those He was teaching. He could do this only because He was so wrapped up in love for them that nothing was repulsive about them. This He said would be the test for these learners when they began to teach. Would they be doing it to establish their own greatness? Then they would hardly be able to wash the feet of their learners. Would they be so in love with one another that nothing seemed repulsive? Then teaching would be an outgrowth of that love.

So there it shows up again. Where does love fit in our teaching relationships? Do we have any love for the teachers who stand before our classes at high school? Is our lack of cooperation with them often just an indication that we haven't taken the trouble to love them? In our family, are teaching and learning going on in all directions? Is a lack of understanding love one of the problems hampering its success? Do parents do this without love, and teen-agers respond without the same? Should we maybe have a good foot-washing session all around just to test out our readiness?

Let's talk about the questions we've just asked.

And let's pray:

Lord Jesus, forgive us our desires to be superior over others. When we try to tell others what to do or when we are being ourselves taught, grant that Your own love may be the setting.

Cursing

We all make mistakes in all kinds of ways, but the man who can claim that he never says the wrong thing can consider himself perfect, for if he can control his tongue, he can control every other part of his personality! Men control the movements of a large animal like the horse with a tiny bit placed in its mouth. Ships too, for all their size and the momentum they have with a strong wind behind them, are controlled by a very small rudder according to the course chosen by the helmsman. The human tongue is physically small, but what tremendous effects it can boast of! A whole forest can be set ablaze by a tiny spark of fire, and the tongue is as dangerous as any fire, with vast potentialities for evil. It can poison the whole body; it can make the whole of life a blazing hell.

Beasts, birds, reptiles, and all kinds of sea creatures can be, and in fact are, tamed by man, but no one can tame the human tongue. It is an evil always liable to break out, and the poison it spreads is deadly. We use the tongue to bless our Father, God, and we use the same tongue to curse our fellowmen, who are all created in God's likeness. Blessing and curses come out of the same mouth — surely, my brothers, this is the sort of thing that never ought to happen! Have you ever known a spring give sweet and bitter water simultaneously? Have you ever seen a fig tree with a crop of olives, or seen figs growing on a vine? It is just as impossible for a spring to give fresh and salt water at the same time. James 3:2-12

Let's face the problem of cursing. We're only kidding if we act as if cursing were no problem around us, aren't we? It would be ridiculous to spell out where cursing is found — it's everywhere. There seems to be a special honor in being a good guy who nevertheless curses. It's manly to curse, fun to curse, exhilarating (at first anyway) to curse. And people expect it. Write a play with no cursing, and it's unrealistic; read a book with no shocking language, and it's too mild. And Christians seem to think of cursing as a sort of exception to their religion.

It certainly ought to be noted that James becomes most vehement and takes the most space when he delivers his volley at cursing. The pages fairly bristle as he talks about the person who can't control his tongue.

"Is it *that* big a problem?" we might ask. Yes, it is. Think of what an important device our tongue is. How often don't we find ourselves having to back up something we've said! We're committed to following through because we spoke, even though it may have been thoughtlessly and carelessly. How true it is that our body doesn't control our tongue — our tongue controls our body! How much of our personality begins to be shaped around the habit of cursing! Our words can give us an attitude of rebellion: "Nobody shoves me around." They can be a front behind which we cover up; they can be a fakery in which we actually deceive ourselves as to just what we are. The tongue is a little member, but it boasts great things. Cursing is serious because our words are so downright important to ourselves and the people around us.

Cursing does God a disservice. "We use the tongue to bless our Father, God, and we use the same tongue to curse our fellowmen, who are all created in God's likeness." Is this the way one of God's creatures should be treated with the words we heap upon him or subject him to hearing? But what about God Himself? The ancient Hebrews would not even mention the name of God out loud, because they didn't want to use it irreverently. How Moses would be shocked to step even into the crowd that gathers in the shadow of the church! "Do these people regard the almighty God so little?" he would wonder. "They can't possibly have any respect for Him."

Nor can cursing be an exception to our religion. It's a fiction to believe that we can be perfectly sincere in our religion but curse profusely. "Have you ever known a spring give sweet and bitter water simultaneously?" James wants to know, as if to say: "Are you going to try to tell me that in your heart there is supreme reverence for your Lord Christ and a complete devotion to Him when on your lips is such treatment for Him?" "A man's words depend on what fills his heart" was the way Jesus analyzed the situation. Cursing is sin just like the other sins and can't be excepted from the need for repentance and change.

But how can we change? Is James right when he declares that no man can tame the tongue? Yes, he is. No *man* can. The only hope for the tongue lies in the heart conquered and ruled by Christ. As Paul puts it: "We take every thought captive to obey Christ, being ready to punish every dis-obedience." Tongue control follows thought control. To let Christ be Lord of our heart is the only way to let Him be

Lord of our tongue. Maybe we need to talk about getting Christ deeper into our hearts.

So let's talk:

> Rather than discuss a set of questions, let's simply talk a few moments about cursing. What can we do about it?

Let's pray:

Lord Jesus Christ forgive us the many, many hurtful words that have proceeded from our lips. Take our hearts captive by Your Holy Spirit that we may serve You with our tongues by speaking only what is acceptable to You and the Father.

Jealousy

Are there some wise and understanding men among you? Then your lives will be an example of the humility that is born of true wisdom. But if your heart is full of rivalry and bitter jealousy, then do not boast of your wisdom — don't deny the truth that you must recognize in your inmost heart. You may acquire a certain superficial wisdom, but it does not come from God — it comes from this world, from your own lower nature, even from the devil. For wherever you find jealousy and rivalry, you will also find disharmony and all other kinds of evil. James 3:13-16

Jealousy doesn't come from God. Such a statement is obvious enough. But before we dismiss it for being so obvious, let's ask where personality traits like this one do come from. We always talk about cause and effect, so what's the cause of jealousy? Looking at these causes will make us take up the responsibility of fighting jealousy in our personality.

James mentions three sources of jealousy. Jealousy comes from "this world." Unfortunately, the human scene is not characterized by the self-giving service of people for one another. Each person lives pretty much for himself and tries to come out at the top of the heap. This will inevitably mean competition — and competition that threatens our own status. Men have a "survival of the fittest" civilization. The good-looking girl gets the handsome fellow and leaves the less attractive envious. The lucky fellow drives the smooth car and leaves the others wishing they were in his seat. How many of our problems of living stem from the fact that the world has much about it which is threatening to us as we see others rise faster than we do, get further, have more! Jealousy is an indication that we do not have the "peace of God" as the overriding human relationship, that we have the self-centeredness of sin.

Jealousy also comes from our own "lower nature." The apostle Paul liked to divide the Christian into "flesh" and "spirit." He was getting at our dual nature. We are born with a nature of selfishness and rebellion. In our baptism, we receive the new nature of the Holy Spirit. So from then on we have both, an "old nature," which is always tending toward selfishness and rebellion, a new one, which is listening to the will of God. The two kinds are in a state of struggle within us. When we are jealous we have let the old nature get the upper hand.

Jealousy finally comes "even from the devil." Satan is a rebel, a powerful one. How people joke about the "friendly little demon"! Yet how we shudder at some of the really horrible crimes of our century! How we wonder why so much of our battle in life is so difficult! Paul knew why: "For our fight is not against any physical enemy: it is against organizations and powers that are spiritual." Satan's mission? To find someone to join his rebellion. So he looks around for something to blow up into sin. Take a harmless little incident in which someone has something we wanted, he blows it up into a full-scale problem. He's like one of those little boys who'd like to see a fight. He hangs around little clusters of boys until he finds something to get them angry at one another and into a full-fledged battle. Jealousy happens when Satan blows a small matter all out of proportion. We get jealous when we let him make something out of it.

But if jealousy doesn't come from God, then that's our answer! Why let the world, our own lower nature, and the devil himself be the only influences in our lives? Why not let God be the overpowering force? It really isn't naive to think this way at all, for God has a way of getting into our personalities, and it's a way that is very available. He has chosen to use the Word and sacraments as His means of entering our lives. So when we are using the Word, God is reaching into us and becoming an influence. When we go to the Lord's Table, the Lord Himself is coming to us in all His might.

Jealousy, rivalry, all other kinds of evil are not caused by God. That's a fact, but it's also an answer.

So let's talk:

How would I be different if I took this passage seriously?
What would I do about it?
Where should I start?

Here's a prayer suggestion:

There are many signs of the influence of the world, our own lower nature, and the devil himself in our lives, O heavenly Father. Forgive us for letting these influences be so predominant, and send us Your Holy Spirit to be a strong force in everything we do, that our lives may reflect You in every way, through Jesus Christ, our Lord.

Wisdom Is Pure

The wisdom that comes from God is first utterly pure. James
3:17

There comes a time when all that we say and learn about
our faith must be put into everyday decisions. All the
sermons about love finally have to end in a decision with
respect to the girl who has just spread some gossip about me.
Now I must decide what I will do. The Bible word for
this is "wisdom," the gift of God to those who are close
to Him. By it we are able to make decisions that are in
line with the faith we possess. It's a pretty exciting thought.
Just as Solomon of old received the gift of God to make
wise decisions about all the cases brought before him, so
we have the gift to make good judgments in the face of the
demands made on us. There are several characteristics of
this gift.

The first is purity. Perhaps we can understand this word
better if we talk about being "unalloyed." A "pure" metal
is one from which every bit of foreign matter has been
supposedly removed. So "pure" gold will have no dirt or
iron or any other material in it. In our day we have learned
how to mix several metals together to form a combination
called an alloy.

Now transfer the picture to the human "heart," the
Bible's word for the center of our personality. What are
it's component parts? An "unalloyed" heart would be one
in which there was nothing but God. That's the way man
was created — "in the image of God." At the center of his
personality was nothing but God. But sinful man has an
alloyed heart, one with all kinds of motives, desires, reasons,
attitudes mixed together. Small wonder that our lives come
out so very complex and we have trouble explaining our
own actions at times!

The characteristic of Christian man is a heart with God

in it again. The Father has regained a place in that heart through Christ. "My son, give me your heart," God says in the Bible, and He is taking it when a person puts his trust in Christ. Because his heart fastens on Christ, his Lord, the Christian has the Holy Spirit dwelling in him.

But the problem of the Christian is all the foreign matter that still remains. God is in the center of our personality again, but not alone. Making an alloy of our hearts are so many desires, attitudes, and characteristics that are completely foreign to God. The challenge of Christian living is thus to get rid of the alloys. If every decision and every action is to come from Him, then the "alloys" must go. Under God's will I decide what to do about a new car, whether or not to go out with this new date, what to do with my life.

So how do I get that kind of purity? "The wisdom that comes from God is first utterly pure." It is a gift from God. But the real "Gift" from God is our Lord Jesus Christ, and He is the One through whom this kind of wisdom comes. He holds out the promise that all who are His receive life and wisdom. But Christ comes to me through the Gospel — written, spoken, contained also in the sacrament. There's no need to withdraw into a monastery. The gift is attainable through Word and sacrament. A pure heart is one which is watching and pondering what God says and replacing its own ideas with the Word of God. This removing of foreign matter and "purifying" of the heart will then be translated into a life of devotion to God.

So let's talk about "unalloyed" hearts:

> Think about the many motives and reasons which lie behind my daily decisions.
> Think about building all actions about God.
> Think about the place of Word and sacrament in this building.
> Now talk about it together.

"Create in me a clean heart, O God, and renew a right spirit within me. Cast me not away from Thy presence, and take not Thy Holy Spirit from me. Restore unto me the joy of Thy salvation, and uphold me with Thy free Spirit."

Wisdom Is Peaceable

The wisdom that comes from God is . . . then peace-loving.
James 3:17

The practical ability to translate Christian faith into everyday decisions is called "wisdom." This wisdom is first "pure," then "peace-loving."

Every day we are bombarded with the absence of peace in human lives. This absence is not just a matter of international tensions. It shows up as one person stabs another. It evidences itself in gangs fighting one another for no good reason. Peace is missing when husband and wife wind up in divorce court ready to renounce the tie that has bound them together. Let's think for a moment of the many levels where peace is so terribly important. And think of what happens when it is missing. Human tragedy is told in the story of elusive peace.

But now let's think of this: The Christian disciple is the messenger of peace! We are directly involved with this personal matter of peace in a community, in a neighbor, or in the world for that matter. One of the severe judgments on the Christian church is that it is not completely identified with peace as Christ certainly meant for it to be. "Blessed are the peacemakers," He said, "for they shall be called the children of God." So as I read those headlines or see that discord or look at this sad lack of peace, I cannot be an innocent spectator. This is my kind of work!

How? The Bible deepens the word "peace" into "being healthy." It sees health not just as a set of physical organs functioning properly but as a personality at peace in itself. Outward explosions are but the results of inner tensions and tragedies. A person who is being driven in many directions inside is not at peace, and he will not be able to live peaceably either. So the greatest need of men is to "have peace" inside, so that they can live peaceably with other men. An unhealthy world situation comes from unhealthy nations; unhealthy nations come from unhealthy people; unhealthy people come from conflicts inside; the conflicts inside come from the sinfulness of our natures, mixed up, misdirected, uncontrolled.

The source of peace is a very specific one. God sends His promised Son, whose one task is to restore man's equilibrium again. As long as God is outside our life, it is out of balance. We were created to have God in the prime spot; without Him we are confused, we are "unhealthy." So down through the centuries before Christ the people read their "headlines," looked sadly at wars, shook their heads at personal tragedies, and looked forward to the day when peace would come. For God had promised He would send a Messiah, and that Messiah would restore peace. "It shall come to pass . . . nation shall not lift up sword against nation . . . and none shall make them afraid." God promised peace through the coming Messiah. So it was only natural that at Bethlehem the angels sang of "peace upon earth." Christ, the Lord, is the Prince of Peace.

But He is the Prince of Peace not as a clever negotiator at the U. N. or a skilled diplomat for world troubleshooting. He is the Prince of Peace as He makes men healthy inside by restoring God as the center of their personalities. His message of peace is: "Repent": change your way of living from self-centeredness and sin to God and His life. He brings peace by bringing the Holy Spirit to take over in the human heart and mind. "Thou wilt keep him in perfect peace whose mind is stayed on Thee" describes the condition of a healthy personality.

If we have this kind of health, then we can be a source of peace for others. In our relations to others we are not full of unfounded fears and anxious threats. The extent to which our personalities are healthy will be the extent to which we can cause peace in our relations to others. And the peace which we have can be spread because the Gospel, which brings it, can be given to others. The Christian church must be concerned about human relationships — it has the Gospel of peace. I must be concerned about human relationships — I have peace.

So let's talk:

How is the peace of God working out in our family?

Is our congregation an avenue of peace?

What would it be doing if it took this seriously?

What should I do about it?

A prayer suggestion:

O God, from whom all holy desires, all good counsels, and all just works do proceed, give unto Thy servants that peace which the world cannot give, that our hearts may be set to obey Thy commandments and that we, being defended by Thee from the fear of our enemies, may pass our time in rest and quietness, through the merits of Jesus Christ, our Savior.

Wisdom Is Gentle

The wisdom that comes from God is . . . gentle. James 3:17

Can gentleness be a trait of Christian character? Is the ability to be gentle one that is "wisdom" — the special gift of God for practical living?

"Gentle" in this passage means "handling people with care." The hospitals have a phrase: "tender loving care." When a patient comes into the hospital, he isn't treated like a piece of human machinery to be repaired. The nurses who practice tender loving care are interested in his loneliness and spend a little time with him. They have respect for his feelings and are willing to explain what's going on. In short, he matters to them, and they treat him like a person.

So the word "gentle" causes us to ask how we "handle" people. We are after all handling lots of people. As we move in and out of our home, we handle the members in it. Does it make any difference if Mom has had a hard day or if teen-age daughter has just lost the man of her dreams or if Dad missed signing that prize customer? How much of our attitudes center in ourselves and what we have a right to expect? Mom should hurry up with dinner, Dad should shell out the allowance, teen-ager should stop being so moody. If it's true that it would be silly to interpret James as saying we ought to handle people with kid gloves, it's just as true that we are to be concerned about the feelings and problems of our family members.

In the same way we handle people in our congregation, our school, our neighborhood, our work. To be able to handle people with care is a gift of God. Our Lord Christ it is who makes us able to see the preciousness of each person in this world. The Pharisees who gleefully drag a sinning woman to Him with their stones ready are dispersed. Jesus says to her: "Neither do I condemn you. Go home and do not sin again." Even the hard and despised criminal hanging on his cross could turn to Jesus and hear: "This very day you will be with Me in Paradise." Every person in the world from monarch to maid took on a precious bearing around Jesus because each was a creature of God. Jesus makes us able to handle people with care because He makes us able to elevate every person, no matter what his job, his appearance, his habits, or his personality, to one of God's creatures.

He makes us able to handle people with care by giving us love to hold in our hearts. "To you whom I love I say, Let us go on loving one another, for love comes from God" was John's way of putting it, and he discusses this love in terms of the way we handle people. Love is an ability given by God for our use. The way we handle people is a test of God's position in our lives.

He enables us to handle people with care by putting such high stakes on the results. There's a good reason for being willing to take time to be concerned about others: We can bring the kingdom of God to them. It is by the way we treat people that they will either be attracted or repulsed. We can win people for the Kingdom or prejudice them against it. Would I ever want my lack of gentleness to stand in the way of Christ's invitation to heaven?

So let's talk:

How would I be different if I took this passage seriously?
How would our family be different?
What difference would it make for my friends?
What difference would it make for God?

Prayer:

Lord Jesus, we know that You care for every person in this world. We know that You died for each one. Forgive us for riding over the feelings of others and being unconcerned about them. Give us the ability to treat them as You do, that we may please You by lives of gentleness.

Wisdom Is Approachable

The wisdom that comes from God is . . . approachable. James
3:17

James wrote his letter in Greek. The word which our trans-
lation calls "approachable" is "easy to be intreated" in the
King James and "open to reason" in the Revised Standard
Version. The dictionary says "obedient."

So let's take our family and find something for both the
parents and the teen-agers. For the parents the word will
be "open to reason" and for the teen-agers "obedient." After
all, aren't these two common complaints: "He never obeys,"
and, "They won't listen to reason"?

God gives the ability to be open to reason. So this is
a feature of the Christian parent. There's no doubt that
God has made me as parent the authority in this home.
There's no doubt that in many ways I can't be running
a democracy — the people just aren't mature enough to
know what's right for them. Many a time, no doubt, I will
have to make a decision which is completely unacceptable
to the teen-ager. I'll have to be ready for some unpopular
reaction. But have I become "unapproachable"? Do I give
my teen-agers any sort of hearing, or do I just go through
the motions of listening to their side of the story? Am I open
to reason?

As a Christian teen-ager I can be obedient. True, I'm
no longer in kindergarten. In many ways my parents don't
understand my generation. They make their mistakes in
judgment. And I have my rights too. But have I stopped
being "obedient"? Do I accept my parents as God's respre-
sentatives, His way of loving and guiding me? Do I ever
raise my cries about democracy and understanding as
a smoke screen for disobedience? Do the problems which
I often blame on my parents really come from my rebellion?
Do I make my parents prove, demonstrate, and guarantee

everything they tell me to do? Am I quick to point out their mistakes when they fail? Am I obedient?

Parents are to be "open to reason." Teen-agers are to be "obedient." But Christ makes us able to combine both into a working relation for our family. The wisdom from above makes us "approachable." The heart of our concern as a Christian family is that we live together. When parents can't approach their teen-agers or teen-agers their parents, there isn't much of a family. This is doubly sad in a Christian family because we are one in Chirst. We serve Him together. Mom and Dad aren't the servants of Christ alone. Each of us is His disciple. That really makes us equals in the family. Not only do we serve together, we are responsible for one another. Cain did not want to be his brother's keeper and was not a good family member. "Carry one another's burdens" is our responsibility as family members. So it's essential for a family to be "approachable." It is our way of living together.

Christ makes us approachable. He puts parents and teen-agers on an equal basis in relation to Him. Both are His disciples. But He spells out that discipleship in terms of always being approachable to others: parents by listening to teen-age voices, teen-agers by being obedient.

So let's talk about it:

Are the members of our family "approachable"?

Do we understand one another?

Where can we improve and help one another?

Our prayer:

Our Father in heaven, we acknowledge that all of us together serve You. Forgive us for the ways we keep others out of our lives, and help us to be approachable to others. Help parents to listen, and help teen-agers to obey, through Jesus Christ.

Wisdom Is Tolerant

The wisdom that comes from God is . . . full of tolerant thoughts and kindly actions. James 3:17

James ties thought and action together in doing good for other people. Very few people refuse to do good for others, but James is concerned with why we help them. The ability to make the action grow out of an inner feeling for someone requires "wisdom" — the practical gift of God. The Pharisees, for example, were great "do-gooders." They made a big deal out of the giving of "alms." They made it such a big deal in fact that they sometimes even had a bugler announce their arrival on the scene. "It's time for my fine work of mercy," the Pharisee was proclaiming. "Oh, how good this makes me feel!" They did many "good" deeds, but their motive was their own enjoyment of being good.

Consider the young woman who became completely upset every Christmas. She hated this festival for all she was worth. As her counselors began to work with her, it developed that she had grown up in an orphanage. There she starved for the love and warmth of a family. But Christmas was the worst time of all, because then crowds of people would come and give big parties with all kinds of gifts. And after the party this perceptive girl saw them depart gaily not to appear again until next year. She did not feel she had been loved but that she had been used. These people had used her to round out their celebration of Christmas. They made themselves feel good by coming, and that was all. She could feel very well that there was no real love flowing from their hearts. Their coming emphasized to her that she was not "people." They treated her as only a thing, "a poor unfortunate," instead of a person.

The "tolerant thoughts" James is talking about are usually translated "mercy" in most versions of the New Testament. But so often mercy can be just what we've described:

a condescending action toward someone. In Christian wisdom the feeling comes first. Christ Himself is mercy in action. When He saw our sin — and sin must look like a terrible need to God — he was not repulsed to the extent of withdrawing to a place where it would not bother Him. But neither was He untouched. He saw us, not just sin. When He looked, He knew our names, He thought of our dreams and our possibilities. As He first of all knew us, He was able to see sin for what it was: a thing to be faced and solved with us. The feeling for us came first, then the decision to do something about our sin.

So there's the punch to "Christian charities." If we turn them into organized goodness on our part, we are joining the Pharisees. No person in this world deserves to be shoved into a class — whether it be a class of unfortunates, handicapped, or retarded. Each person in this world deserves first of all to be a person with a name, with problems, with dreams, with feelings. Christ doesn't just want to know what we've done for people; He wants to know how we've loved them. And love is as practical as knowing a person's name, giving him some chance to be a person.

Heartless "charities" are the worst kind. Obviously we will support our wonderful institutions of mercy. They do what we could not do individually. But that's the only reason we support them — not to substitute for any concern on our part and certainly not to get rid of our obligation. For our personal lives we still need to be looking for those opportunities to link thoughts of feeling with actions of kindness.

So let's talk:

> Let's talk about the kind of "charity" we practice. Is it adequate when looked at through Christ's definition? How can we change?

Our prayer:

Fill our hearts with loving interest in the people we meet, Holy Spirit, especially those who have a special need for our help. Keep us from treating them like things, and preserve us from helping them simply for our own conceit. Give us the attitude of our Lord Jesus Christ.

Wisdom Allows No Favoritism

The wisdom that comes from God is first utterly pure . . . with no breath of favoritism or hint of hypocrisy. James 3:17

Can it be true that having favorites is inconsistent with Christian discipleship? Surely it can't be wrong to like one person more than another! Actually "favoritism" doesn't quite come out that way. What James is getting at is partiality, the deliberate exclusion of someone from what he deserves, be it our help, our love, or anything else.

Favoritism is hypocrisy for a Christian. It is hypocrisy because of the claims which a Christian makes. The prime characteristic of the disciple is that he practices love. The really different feature of this love, though, is that it is not limited in any way to certain people. "If you love those who love you, what reward have you? . . . And if you salute only your brethren, what more are you doing than others? . . . You therefore must be perfect, as your heavenly Father is perfect." Favoritism denies the all-inclusiveness of Christian love, and therefore it's hypocrisy to claim to be a Christian while playing favorites.

But that makes all of us hypocrites! Who could stay free from that kind of charge? It's just this realization that gives us a better insight into our Christian life. It is not possible to sort out life into sins and virtues and assume that Christianity lies in doing a good job of sorting. The truth is that sin lives in us as a force. It colors our activities and influences our decisions. "If we say that we have no sin, we deceive ourselves, and the truth is not in us." So the answer to favoritism is hardly: "Well, now that I know it's sin, it won't appear again in my life." The people who give this answer are sure to be frustrated and will be hypocrites too. They deceive themselves into thinking they have eliminated sin.

Rather the finding of favoritism in us should lead in a different direction. As the doctor uses a hacking cough, high temperature, and red spots to diagnose measles, so we use such things as favoritism and jealousy to look deeper at what we really are. And what we find is that we are people whom the Lord Christ is not ruling fully. His redemption freed us from being slaves to sin, but now there's the matter of His being Ruler of our life from the inside out. Without Him the pattern is stamped by selfishness, favoritism, and all other sins. But because we are His, the pattern being formed is a new one. It is the pattern of His own self. A Christian is starting to turn out like Christ. He's turning out that way because that's the pattern the Holy Spirit is using to rebuild Him. And when we see things like favoritism in our personalities, we see the job the Holy Spirit has in hammering out the new pattern.

So the result of seeing favoritism is to ask ourselves about the rule of Christ. Was my turning a cold shoulder the other day out of character with Christ? Can it be that I won't invite this person to my parties because I'm not willing to bring my attitudes under the rulership of Christ? Do my habits of picking and choosing indicate a lack for me, a lack of the completeness of Christ's rule? And if they do, I know what must come next.

So let's talk:

Discuss the questions in the last paragraph.

Now think about how we might bring this area of life under Christ too.

Our prayer:

Continue to live in our hearts, Lord Jesus Christ, that we may root out all habits which are unworthy of us as Your disciples. Remove our insincerity and hypocrisy, and warm us to the joy of serving You fully.

Righteousness

And the wise are peacemakers who go on quietly sowing for a harvest of righteousness — in other people and in themselves.
James 3:18

Speed down a highway and wind up in front of the judge. Do nothing all quarter and get a bad grade. Or to put it in old, old, words: "As you sow, so shall you reap." The focus now is on righteousness. Where does it fit our lives? That if we are good, we will be happy? That sounds kind of sugary for James. There must be more to it.

There is. In fact, we can't start thinking about righteousness until we know that God has to give it. Righteousness is more than a few nice deeds or a couple of good days. No one is "good" in the real sense of the word, because good doesn't mean abstaining from a few obviously bad habits. Righteousness and goodness are big words, including all of God and all of life in a healthy working personality. So we can't possibly be righteous on our own. Nobody is that way.

But neither can we set up righteousness on our own. Those who do are the phonies of our day. They are the ones who are proud of the things they don't do, make much of the golden rule as being a perfect religion, and assume that they are better than others. None of us likes a phony, and above all we don't like people who are phony about being righteous. Yet if we set out to be righteous just by observing rules we will come out phony. Our good deeds will only make our bad ones look worse.

That's why Jesus said: "Blessed are those who hunger and thirst for righteousness" (RSV). Hunger and thirst are cravings for something, desire for it. We don't satisfy hunger and thirst by imagining we are full or by going through the motions of chewing or by looking at pictures of food. We satisfy them only when there is food and we can have it. The person who hungers and thirsts after righteousness is the one who knows it will have to be given him. The mark of a disciple of Jesus is not first of all that he *does* righteousness but that he *desires* it. It is the work of God already when we realize that the only way we will be righteous is if He provides it.

But the joy of the Christian life is that God gives it. In Jesus Christ we receive status as the righteous children of God. He forgives us and establishes us as full-fledged members of His household, participating in all its characteristics. And one of these characteristics is righteousness, being upright and righteous before God.

So because we have received righteousness from God, we can talk about using it in our lives. We can take what we receive and do wonderful things with it. God pours into us His righteousness, and we live out that righteousness in our world. We live peaceably with people, we witness to the Lord Jesus Christ, we help those in need. In all kinds of ways we can sow it in our daily lives.

And the harvest will be one of righteousness. The righteousness sown in our lives will bear fruit for us and others. Some will be led to God, others will come closer. But all of us will reap the joy of being before God and seeing the results of our labors.

Many lives are wasted lives because they never really

sow anything. They are just a mess of activities. Many Christians waste their blessings because they don't do anything with them. We can sow for a harvest of righteousness and thus be people with the "wisdom that comes from God."

So let's talk:

> Is my life headed in any specific direction?
>
> How does "sowing for a harvest of righteousness" apply to me?
>
> How would I be different if I took this seriously?

Prayer:

We thank You, Lord Jesus Christ, for making us righteous before God, our Father. We confess that without it we would have nothing on which to stand before Him. Now we pray You to send Your Holy Spirit that we may sow this righteousness into our way of living and in the end reap the harvest to Your glory.

Those Things We Want

But what about the feuds and struggles that exist among you — where do you suppose they come from? Can't you see that they arise from conflicting passions within yourselves? You crave for something and don't get it; you are jealous and envious of what others have got and you don't possess it yourselves. Consequently, in your exasperated frustration you struggle and fight with one another. You don't get what you want because you don't ask God for it. And when you do ask, He doesn't give it to you, for you ask in quite the wrong spirit — you want only to satisfy your own desires. James 4:1-3

Our civilization is pretty well based on "getting." Who doesn't have desires which he is trying to satisfy, and who would deny that these desires lie behind all his activity?

Can we deny that it's in our desires that we show some of the deepest marks of sin? Our very strivings to have are loaded with the dangers of sin. In fact, the Bible has a word for the psychology of our motives. It talks about "self-centered" desires. The problem is not that we have desires but that these desires are centered on us to the exclusion of other men and of God. This self-centeredness is what makes them sins.

Look at the results. On the world level there are wars because there are nations striving to satisfy themselves with no concern for the results of their aggression. On the personal level there are conflicts of all kinds between people because of their self-centered desires. Each is striving to satisfy only himself, and when two persons wanting the same thing meet, there is trouble.

But now here's the real problem. We children of God are not free from this kind of battle. It is very true that the Holy Spirit is leading us to listen to the voice of God, but it is also true that we have a basic personality which is self-centered. And what happens then? Prayer is abused. How often prayer is condensed into a sort of hoped-for TV program in which our secret dreams will be realized! And how often we limit our prayers to asking for things we want! So James says "you pray and you don't receive" because to give to you would just be to let you remain captive to your desires.

And when we stop to think of it, that isn't the Christian life at all. Christianity is not magic for getting your way. Jesus Christ came to reestablish our relation to God, our Father. It follows, then, that the essence of Christian living will be the keeping and deepening of that relation. In the last analysis it's not really the "things" of life that are so all-fired important; it's what we do with them. Are they in harmony with our faith relationship to God — or do they detract from it? Our desires will either lead us to God, or they will lead us away from Him. Our greatest need in life is that God take our very desires captive.

And so our prayers are not push-button magic, or instant shopping. They are the conversation of a disciple seeking to understand and obey His master's will. It's true that we come to our Father with all kinds of desires, problems, requests and thoughts. But the result of our praying is that we will have brought these practical situations under our Father's will. How we pray is an indication of our Christian life. Let's talk about our desires and our prayers.

Let's talk:

Can I take a good look at my desires?

Can I talk with God about them?

Am I prepared to hear His answer?

Let's pray:

Our Father in heaven, we know that we are full of desires for all kinds of things. We bring these desires to You. Help us to abandon the things that are hurtful to us and to ask only the things that are pleasing to You; through Jesus Christ, our Lord.

World vs. God

You are like unfaithful wives, flirting with the glamor of this world and never realizing that to be the world's lover means becoming the enemy of God! Anyone who deliberately chooses to love the world is thereby making himself God's enemy. Do you think what the Scriptures have to say about this is a mere formality? Or do you imagine that this spirit of passionate jealousy is the Spirit He has caused to live in us? No, He gives us grace potent enough to meet this and every other evil spirit if we are humble enough to receive it. That is why He says:

God resisteth the proud
But giveth grace to the humble. James 4:4-6

Is it wrong to enjoy this life? Are we in trouble just because we love this world? Must I go through life feeling just a little guilty because I am not anxiously waiting for heaven? What can we say about "World vs. God" in the Bible?

We'd better start with understanding what "world" does not mean to James. It certainly does not mean "what God created." When God looked at His world at the end of His creation, "it was very good." God could hardly hate what He had made! And if God doesn't hate it, why should we?

So what is the problem? The problem is what we make "world" to be. We do the very thing which seems unthinkable: we separate God from His world and then love the result! The Creator is removed from His creation, the Ruler from His kingdom, the Giver from His gift to us. We take what God created, then shove Him out of the picture, and the "world" becomes a sad thing indeed. Now instead of being God's creation and life, the meaning of "world" becomes rebellion and death. Systems rage back and forth across the world quite out of harmony with God or His life, and they are definitely at war with God.

And here's the point: We can fall in love with this kind of "world." The glitter of its activity, the lure of its sins, and the promises of its plans are exciting and attractive. So the result is that we become people who forget God to fall head over heels in love with "world," the entire system and activity which is set against Him. "Anyone who deliberately chooses to love the world is thereby making himself God's enemy." And there's the tragedy for a person.

How can we then live in the world without making it the enemy of God? "He gives us grace potent enough to meet this and every other evil spirit if we are humble enough to receive it." The grace is centered in Christ, who came to make us God's people again, not confined to a world without Him. It is grace that delivered us and restored us to God so that He is not only part of "world" again but the dominant part. It is grace that continues to flow through our lives in the person of the Holy Spirit, who lives right in us. That's the kind of people we are: people full of grace; people therefore with a view of life and world which has God at the center; people full of love for God and man.

The challenge for us, then, is to live in this grace. We take advantage of it as we keep building our attitudes, our ambitions, our loves around it. We are "humble enough to receive it" when our prayers and our planning draw fully on this kind of grace and leave plenty of room for God in us. The Lord Christ carefully laid the groundwork of this kind of life for us. He came to restore "life" to us, the real life centered in God. To have Christ's life is to love God, and to live it out is to be concerned about God. Our prayers, our worship, our use of God's Word are all aspects of this "life" being lived with God at the center again. With this kind of basic view we are able to constantly reshape our attitude about the world and keep on getting rid of sin.

So "love not the world" is finally going to have to be a matter resolved in Christ.

Let's talk about it:

> Are we willing to measure the world, or do we simply love it blindly?
>
> Is God central in our lives?
>
> Do we grasp the full meaning of being disciples in this life?
>
> Can we see too many compromises in our lives?
>
> What does grace mean to us?

Let's pray:

Our heavenly Father, teach us through Jesus Christ to enjoy Your creation without falling in love with it, to appreciate Your material gifts without becoming greedy over them, to live in Your world without putting You out of it.

Resisting Things

Be humble then before God. But resist the devil and you'll find he'll run away from you. James 4:7

The word James uses for "resist" implies a deliberate action on our part. It brings us to the question, "To what extent am I responsible for staying free from sin?" A rather appealing thought is to say, "Not at all. No one can stay free from sin, and therefore I can't be blamed when I happen to fall." But that's not quite true.

Our Lord Jesus Christ never indicated that His death would make us free from responsibility before God. Quite the contrary; He made it very clear that His coming to a person demands some real personal decisions which had better not be ignored. "No one sets out to build a house without first counting the cost," He said. And the cost is quite specific: "Repent." The repentance is specific too. It involves turning from sin and the love of it to God and the love of Him. It means: "Change your mind." John the Baptist drew in bold outline what the change meant for people. For tax collectors it meant: "Collect no more than is appointed you." For soldiers: "Rob no one by violence, and be content with your wages." Our conversion must be translated into a decision about sin, or it isn't conversion.

And for us who have made this decision, discipleship is translated into our everyday struggle with sin, or it is no discipleship. We translate it into resistance. The Bible assumes that we will all our lives be offered opportunities to sin. The places we frequent, the things we do with the crowd, all our personal activities will require responsible effort on our part. "The devil prowls around like a roaring lion, seeking someone to devour." Now, it's true that the Lord Jesus Christ has fought the devil and conquered Him. It's also true that this victory assures us that we do not have to become the devil's slaves. But it's also true that our own decision in all this must be to obey God and resist the devil. That's the basic decision of Christian discipleship.

So we need to put it into practice. We have the grace of God poured into our lives. Must this be used simply for forgiveness after we have fallen? Or can't it be a building block of our personal character? The grace of God is finally this, that through the Gospel the Holy Spirit begins to live in us, pouring in His strength and understanding all the time. This means that we have the strength to make decisions to resist sin. It just isn't true that "we couldn't help it." Christ set us on the path of discipleship — a path which presupposes our responsible backbone.

In fact, James very nicely points out that we resist either the devil or God. The devil's pressure encourages us to "go ahead this time." The Holy Spirit asks us to obey. So we'll have to resist one and obey the other. We can think of many times when we resist God. "Why must I worship? Don't take so much of my money! Why do I have to love that neighbor?" When we thus resist God, we're giving in to the devil. But when do we resist Satan? "Don't go in there! Don't believe that gossip! Watch that temper!" When we thus resist Satan, we're obeying God.

God gives us His grace — His grace to use. When we pray for His help in withstanding temptation, we commit ourselves to making decisions against that temptation.

So let's talk:

> Do I really mean it when I ask God to help me fight temptation?
>
> Do I intend to make any effort to do so?
>
> Why would I rather not think about this?

Let's pray:

Our Father in heaven, we confess that we would often prefer not to listen to You. Grant us grace to obey You and resist the devil. Forgive us our failures, and strengthen us in our struggle against temptation and sin; through Christ, our Lord.

Approaching God

Come close to God and He will come close to you. Realize that you have sinned, and get your hands clean again. Realize that you have been disloyal, and get your hearts made true once more. As you come close to God, you should be deeply sorry, you should be grieved, you should even be in tears. Your laughter will have to become mourning, your high spirits will have to become heartfelt dejection. You will have to feel very small in the sight of God before He will set you on your feet once more. James 4:8-10

What does God think when He sees me? Imagine me kneeling there in prayer. I wonder what He thinks. There I stand, taking Communion. What does He see in me? It almost makes me squirm just to think of God in such a personal way. But let's go on with it.

He sees my hands, symbolic of my activities. What's in them? Put all my activities into my hands, and bring them to Him. What do I bring? Cruel words to my family yesterday; cheating on my test this morning; jealousy about the neighbor's new car; stinginess in my offering envelope. What a list I could compile! Can I actually be such a sinner? I usually think of myself as a really decent person. But when I come to God, is there so much to brag about? Isn't there a great deal to be sorry about?

But that brings up my heart. He sees my heart, symbolic of my loyalty, and what He sees really makes me shudder. He sees that I'm really not very sorry for my sins. I may try to act as if I believed I'm a sinner, but deep down inside it's pretty hard for me to accept. The truth of the matter is that most of the time I'm not very concerned about how God feels; I'm more wrapped up in living it up to the hilt. So there I stand before Him, hands full of sins, heart divided between the sins and Him.

How small I feel when I look at it this way! I don't even mean all the things I sing and talk about. And when it comes to what God must think of me, I hate even to talk about it.

Maybe we should close our thoughts right here. Maybe we should let ourselves feel good and small once, really humble. Maybe then we wouldn't rush so quickly from our little encounter with God right back to sin again. Maybe so.

But maybe I can do something even better. Maybe I can use this vantage point to understand Christ for a change. When I stop to think of it, has Christ really been the answer to anything in my life? Hasn't it been true that I've been content to try to master many teachings about Him and to be as interested in Him as I can? But after I have done this, hasn't it also been true that I still felt a little funny about the whole thing? Hasn't the thought of a person dying on a cross as my "Savior from sin" left me wondering a little about God's arithmetic, and even more about why God should find all this necessary? Haven't I wondered why all the trouble?

And now it hits me! I can't really appreciate Christ, because I don't really appreciate myself. When I'm feeling small and sinful, the cross of Christ is a tremendous comfort to me. Somehow the questions about God's arithmetic don't seem as important. Then I'm just full of gratitude that God tells me I don't have to go hang my head and give up. It's when I feel small that I know what Christ is all about, for He's the answer to my smallness. Whether this was the best way or the only way God could accept me doesn't become the issue. The point is, God does accept me for Jesus' sake. I can ask myself, Did Christ die on that cross? And I can answer, Yes. Then I ask, Was my sinfulness the reason He died? And I can answer Yes to that too. And there I have it, the real story of my faith, from my smallness to God's love.

What happens when I come close to God and He comes close to me? I hope I will always realize that I am a sinner, for then in my smallness I'm ready for God to exalt me, to show me Christ.

Let's talk:

How do I feel when I confess my sins in church?
What does Christ mean to me?
Must I feel my sin to appreciate Christ?

Our prayer:

Our Father in heaven, we confess that sin occupies much of our life and that we feel small about it only when we realize what You think of it. Forgive us our smallness through Jesus Christ, Your Son, our Lord, who died just for people like us.

Tearing Others Apart

Never pull one another to pieces, my brothers. If you do, you are judging your brother and setting yourself up in the place of God's Law; you have become in fact a critic of the Law. Yet if you start to criticize the Law instead of obeying it, you are setting yourself up as judge, and there is only one Judge, the one who gave the Law, to whom belongs absolute power of life and death. How can you then be so silly as to imagine that you are your neighbor's judge? James 4:11, 12

Perhaps one of the most telling indications of how deeply sin influences our character is the pleasure we gain from tearing someone apart. It's almost impossible not to get a certain delight from hearing something unfavorable about even our best friends. We certainly have often been glad to find out something wrong about a person we don't like. It's a subtle, almost unnoticed fault of our personality to rather enjoy tearing others apart.

The implications of doing this must be given. When we begin to pull at each other, we are criticizing God's way of doing things. God has replaced a cold, hard set of rules with the law of love. The operating principle of this law is that we do not draw up a minute set of rules which make a person Christian and then proclaim him unbeliever when he breaks one. To put it at its bluntest, it just isn't so, that the staid, unimaginative spinster can huff up her sterling character at the fellow who's having his troubles with the bottle and assume that he can't be as good as she who has kept the rules. The Lord of love is not dealing with a minimum set of requirements as His guide to discipleship. He is concerned about the direction a person is going. How great a judgment stands against our preaching of Christianity when a person feels he isn't good enough to receive our message!

But even more serious: our picking at others replaces God in our lives. There is one Judge, the one who gave the law, and His power in fact reaches to the granting of life and death. We all stand under Him. How very important that every man everywhere be concerned about his standing in that Judge's eyes and in no other's. But when we start to judge someone, we are no longer looking at that responsibility. We have climbed into God's place. We aren't willing to be the ones being judged — we want to judge! Because we're looking at someone else's weakness, it becomes difficult to see our own. What God thinks is not as important as what we think. To judge someone else is to ignore God's place in our lives.

So the net result of tearing someone else apart is that we are judging ourselves. We show that we are pushing God away from the center of our own lives and letting our self-centered human nature take over. Symptoms such as these can lead to only one Physician. We need help, not for our friends but for ourselves. The help we need is for God's kind of law to operate in us, the kind that doesn't get excited about a standard brand of goodness by which we can judge. We need rather the kind that builds people up — starting wherever they are. We need, in other words, "the mind of Christ." The Christian life is constantly being reshaped by the mind of Christ. It just isn't possible to let Him be our Savior without Him coming right into our personalities. We are His in more ways than one. And one of the results of His mind in us will be the ability to build people up instead of tearing them down.

So let's talk:

How would I be different if I took this seriously?

What difference would it make among my friends?

How would it help?

Our prayer:

Our Father in heaven, we thank You for the new life given us in our Lord Jesus Christ. Now help us to live that life by applying love and fellowship to others without the smallness of petty and unjust criticism.

What Is My Life

Just a moment, now, you who say: "We are going to such-and-such a city today or tomorrow. We shall stay there a year doing business and make a profit"! How do you know what will happen even tomorrow? What, after all, is your life? It is like a puff of smoke visible for a little while and then dissolving into thin air. Your remarks should be prefaced with, "If it is the Lord's will, we shall still be alive and shall do so-and-so." As it is, you get a certain pride in yourself in planning your future with such confidence. That sort of pride is all wrong.
James 4:13-16

When has a Christian really begun to show the effect of God's work in his life? How does it show up in his attitude toward life?

Some people's Christianity amounts to: "I'd better believe or I'll be lost." Such an attitude is of course one of fear. In such a person there is a great danger involved, and that danger dominates all of his thinking. But fear isn't what Christ came to establish! One could hardly say that this person is now living out the fullness of Christ's work. Fear can come from all kinds of places; to be afraid we'll be lost can hardly be the epitome of our life. True, we need to realize the dire consequences of unbelief. But if my religion is strictly a result of fear, fear for my neck, the full light of God has hardly come to me yet.

Others make the matter just a bit more positive. "God will take me to heaven when I die." Now that sounds fine, but many people reduce life to no more than that. Their religion becomes a very selfish thing finally: the prime need is to get *me* saved. If I must go to church, I will do that; if I must support the Kingdom, I will do that; if I must refrain from certain habits, I will do that. But all of this is centered on *me* and on getting *me* to heaven.

The problem of this kind of religion, you see, is that the emphasis is on me instead of God. God fits, but not as God, as the One who is more important than myself. My approach to life, then, is not: "if the Lord wills," but: "if the Lord agrees." I don't give much thought to God getting His way in all of my life — I've consigned Him to only one area. In the other areas I follow my own will, and hope for His agreement.

But where does God bring us in our attitude toward life? A look at Old Testament Israel will give us a telling illustration. God let Israel wander in the wilderness for 40 years. Was He doing this simply because He was angry? Was He simply dealing out the amount of punishment they had earned? Moses saw the matter a lot more clearly. Right before Israel entered the new land, in his farewell speech, Moses put his finger on it. "He humbled you . . . that you might know that man does not live by bread alone but by every word that proceeds from the mouth of God." The real reason for the 40 years was that of preparation. Israel was God's chosen nation, His servant to the rest of the world. So Israel was to be the leader, already practicing what all men should come to know: that our lives do not continue because we find food every day or because our lungs have so much air still left in them but because God is saying, "Live." This is the view of life that is the result of God's activity in us.

I exist because God is saying, "Live." Just as the stars shine and the waters roll as a result of God's "let there be," so I am living because God is saying I shall. I cannot separate "religion" and "life," because life itself is God's affair. I cannot reduce God's activity to heaven, for life here on earth is the result of His direct involvement with me. When God's work really bears fruit in me, all my life will be lived under His providence. I will see life and God always together. I know that I will get up tomorrow or take that trip or make this goal "if the Lord wills."

With this view of life, the Lord's will is absolutely essential. Without His will there will be no life. It only follows that I seek His will and ask His blessing for all of life's details. In my plans, my activities, my dreams I will consciously say, "If the Lord wills."

Israel in the wilderness was taught the hard way. In our case the Lord Jesus went outside the city to the hard place of Calvary to work the same results in us. There He "reconciled" men to God; He brought them together again. We are able to accept our entire life from God because we have a new kind of will, one shaped by the Holy Spirit.

We are showing the result of His work when we live our life "if the Lord wills."

So let's talk:

Is my "religion" separate from my life?

Do I tend to live "by bread alone"?

Do I take God's providence into consideration in my ideas for the future?

Let's pray:

Our heavenly Father, we know that our life comes from You and is completely dependent on You. We confess that we often forget You completely as we rush to live our daily lives. Restore Your place within us that all things may be done under Your benediction and by Your permission, through Jesus Christ, our Lord.

Ingredients of Our Lives

No doubt you agree with the above in theory. Well, remember that if a man knows what is right and fails to do it, his failure is a real sin. James 4:17

Let's spend this meditation thinking about the "ingredients" which have gone into making us disciples of Christ. Let's do this so that we will accept fully our position as Christ's people, in no way content to be just like everyone else or to reduce our faith to theory without practice.

Let's think first of our baptism. Was this just some incident in our past history? Apparently the apostle Paul doesn't think so. When people ask him if it's all right to keep on sinning since we'll be forgiven anyway, he replies, "By no means! How can we who died to sin still live in it? Do you not know that all of us who have been baptized into Christ Jesus were baptized into his death? We were buried therefore with Him by baptism into death, so that as Christ was raised from the dead by the glory of the Father, we too might walk in newness of life. . . . Let not sin therefore reign in your mortal bodies." I have been personally baptized into my Lord Jesus Christ; my life and the life of an unbaptized person certainly come from different sources. Must this not make a difference?

Then there's our Christian instruction. What has been my particular history? Have I been taught from childhood about Christ, or did I first begin to learn as a teen-ager or adult? The Holy Scriptures are "able to make you wise to salvation through faith which is in Christ Jesus" and are given that the "man of God may be complete, ready for every good work." Has the pouring in of Scripture into my life had any noticeable result? Is this ingredient showing up in the finished product?

And then what about the Lord's Supper? I go to the Communion rail to take the heavenly food, and I hear the words "given and shed for you for the remission of sins." Can a person who has come that close to Christ be just an ordinary sinner like everyone else? Must not such strengthening of my faith result in a strengthening of my Christian life? If my life is disappointing to me, would this be because I am not giving sufficient attention to the Lord's Table as well as to the Scriptures?

When I stop to think of it, I represent a lot of work on God's part. I always knew there was a tremendous task involved for Christ. He spent 33 years on earth and finally died on the cross for me. But what about all those ways of bringing Him here to me? Are they to be meaningless? Can I let them all operate in my life without results? Others may sin for no good reason, but when I do, I'm going against a lot of basic ingredients in my life.

So I especially need God's forgiveness — forgiveness for letting the results of his work be so small in me. I need to be forgiven for giving myself to the same old goals and greeds as anyone else in spite of the life which is in me through baptism. I need forgiveness for acting as if I knew nothing about loving my neighbor and keeping God's name holy and about the temporariness of this world's "glitter" when I've had so much of Holy Scripture to tell me otherwise. I need to be forgiven my lack of love when I've partaken of the Lord's feast to be strengthened in my Christian life.

I need forgiveness, and I need God's gift. He must keep using these very means to change me. They are all effective ways of working in me. But when He works, it becomes my task to put them into practice. This is the exciting challenge of my Christian discipleship, not just to agree in theory, but to put it into practice.

So let's talk:

> Is baptism a power in my present life or just past history?
>
> How is the Bible faring in my life?
>
> What does the Lord's Supper mean to me?
>
> To what extent do I accept the challenge of putting my faith into practice?

Let's pray:

O Holy Spirit, we know that You work in each of us through the Word and the sacraments. Forgive us our hardness which lets us neglect these gifts in our actual lives. Continue to come to us through them, and when You come, grant that we put into practice the faith that lives in us; through Jesus Christ, our Lord.

Using Money

And now, you plutocrats, is the time for you to weep and moan because of the miseries in store for you! Your richest goods are ruined; your hoard of clothes is moth-eaten; your gold and silver are tarnished. Yes, their very tarnish will be the evidence of your wicked hoarding, and you will shrink from them as if they were red-hot. You have made a fine pile in these last days, haven't you? But look, here is the pay of the reaper you hired and whom you cheated, and it is shouting out against you! And the cries of the other laborers you swindled are heard by the Lord of Hosts Himself. Yes, you have had a magnificent time on this earth and have indulged yourselves to the full. You have picked out just what you wanted like soldiers looting after battle. You have condemned and ruined innocent men in your career, and they have been powerless to stop you. James 5:1-6

It would be hard to find a place where the love of riches is more soundly denounced. Is James justified in being so harsh? Can the love of a few things really be that bad? We have quite a few possessions. What should be our approach to them? We won't understand James's severity until we look at a few words — words like steward, money, and indulgence.

Let's start with "steward." Any talk about giving money to God will be small and petty if it begins with us and our needs. The real beginning of the story must be at a crude cross on a Friday afternoon many years back. There a real gift of grace was being given. "You know the grace of our Lord Jesus Christ, that though He was rich, yet for your sake He became poor." There He hangs — He who knew the complete comfort of heaven, feeling the splinters of the wood; He who knew the absolute reverence of angels themselves, taking the abuse of common soldiers; He who held in His power the ability to give life, dying. The cross is the only vantage point from which to look at our lives, because our lives are so completely marked by this gift. We are stewards because we have been made His people by that gift. It's His kingdom. It's His earth. It always has been. But we are His people working in His kingdom with His earth to fulfill His plan that men may be saved.

So let's look at the next word — "money." The Lord Christ didn't say, "Now that I've saved you, let's get out of here." If we went to India, we would find the noblest person to be the one most out of touch with life. He's the beggar who has separated himself from any concern about house, clothes, or things. He has almost escaped this life; he's completely out of touch. But we don't have to leave this earth to start living. We are started right now. Our task is not to escape house, food, and things but to use them. We are stewards: people who *use* these for our Lord. In our country this life is in so many aspects reduced to coin. Our work results in a paycheck, our house depends on house payments or rent, our food is purchased with dollars. So money is the key to operating with the things we are using as stewards.

And that brings us to the third word — "indulge." To indulge ourselves is to take what God places in our care and waste it on ourselves. These are the "plutocrats" James is talking about, those who have forgotten they are stewards and are having a grand time devoting everything to themselves. What a tremendous waste when God's gift is ignored and God's possessions are thrown around helter-skelter to no purpose but our own satisfaction!

Now, the trouble is that we can't just divide the world into plutocrats and stewards. In each of us exists the tendency to both. We want to be God's stewards, yet we also like to indulge in things without regarding God. That's why hammering out a working approach to money is the task of each Christian, teen-ager or parent. It's as practical a matter as setting up a budget to show ourselves why we can spend money as we do on recreation, food, and car. It's also as necessary as deciding what proportion is going to be set aside for God *first*.

So let's talk:

Does our family have a stewardship budget?

Can we talk about it?

Am I as a teen-ager practicing stewardship — or indulgence?

Do we enjoy being stewards?

Our prayer:

We thank you, Father, for entrusting so many things to our stewardship. We ask Your forgiveness for often using these selfishly instead of devoting them to You and Your service. Enable us by Thy Holy Spirit to use all our possessions in harmony with Your will; through Jesus Christ, our Lord.

The Lord Will Come

But be patient, my brothers, as you wait for the Lord to come. Look at the farmer quietly awaiting his precious harvest. See how he has to possess his soul in patience till the land has had the early and late rains. So must you be patient, resting your hearts on the ultimate certainty. The Lord's coming is very near. James 5:7, 8

It's very true that our Christian faith is part of our daily life. We are not walking around with tickets to heaven and no interest in what is happening on earth. But it's also true that there is always an unfinished aspect to our Christian life.

The unfinished part comes from Jesus Himself. After He had risen from the dead and before He ascended into heaven, He told the disciples to keep working till He returned. *The Day* must have been a very important part of their thinking as they lived and worked always ready for His return. They surely must have gotten the point when Jesus told them all those stories about a king going off to a far country and leaving his servants behind with the work. They knew good and well whom He meant when He said,

"Blessed is that servant whom his lord, when he cometh, shall find so doing." So Christianity has always had this unfinished nature about it: it will not reach its climax until the Lord keeps that promise and returns to earth. We, the spiritual descendants of the disciples, are living "till He come."

This tie to the future is really the anchor of our faith. Just as a ship has an anchor to keep it securely stationed in the right place, our hope is in the heavens, tied to the Lord Christ. "So must you be patient, resting your hearts on the ultimate certainty. The Lord's coming is very near." This hope is our mainstay in life and will culminate in seeing Him at the Last Day.

This hope, then, has important implications for us. One implication is that our goals will certainly be longer-range. Those who have no vision beyond the grave are going to have shortsighted goals. Getting to the moon or making a mint or becoming the finest doctor look like pretty long-range goals when the grave is the last stage in life. But if it's true that the Lord Christ will return again, then any goal short of His approval will be less than worthwhile. People live by goals, and people show their idea of life by their goals. Does the coming of Christ shape our goals?

The return of our Lord also shapes our sense of values. Before they met Jesus, the disciples had a different set of values. On the one hand they longed for the redemption of Israel, but on the other it seemed very important to them to be fishing or collecting taxes, or whatever their occupation. After His ascension they were driven by a whole new sense of values. Money and possessions had a very minor role in their lives, as did a lot of other things. Now the most valuable possession was the Word which had been committed to them, and the most important work became the sharing of that Word. If we are looking for Jesus to return again, our system of values will reflect it.

And there was a difference in their accomplishments. We were never told how successful a fisherman Peter was after the ascension or how good a tentmaker Paul was. All we know is that they must have preached thousands of times and spent hours calling on people. Their works were to bring the Kingdom to men. They wanted people ready for the return of their Lord. How about our activities of the past month? Are there any works which are devoted to preparation for His return?

"Patient waiting" is a real challenge for Christs's disciples. It means more than half-hearted resignation to the idea that Christ will come again. It means having the kind of hard look at life which deliberately lets our values, attitudes, and accomplishments be centered in the return of Christ. And it means keeping them that way through 10, 20, or 80 years. A farmer puts the seed into the ground and doesn't have anything to show for it over weeks and even months. But comes the harvest and his work proves itself — it was a good idea to sow. Often there's little that we can demonstrate to others as the "advantage" of being Christ's disciples. But we don't need to. Our home is completely centered in the day when Christ returns and we will see the realization of our goals — really long-range ones, really worthwhile ones.

So let's talk:

> Do our goals have any connection with our Lord's return?
> How about our system of values?
> How about our activities?
> What about our vocation in life?

Let's pray:

> Remove from our hearts all shortsightedness and lack of vision, Lord Jesus Christ, that when You come again we may be found living in readiness for You.

Complaints

Don't make complaints against one another in the meantime, my brothers — you may be the one at fault yourself. The Judge Himself is already at the door. James 5:9

Does this family sit down to have "roast preacher" for Sunday dinner? The main thrust of James's words about complaints seems to be within the church, so let's think specifically about our congregation.

What kind of treatment does our pastor get? Do we see him as unable to keep us awake with his sermons? Are we quick to point out how little he understands teen-agers? Is Dad quite sure this congregation would really get going under a different man? But let's stop to think further. How did he get to our congregation? Don't we believe that God sent him to us? When our congregation met, it prayed that God would guide them in their election and then voted for one man out of several. Didn't God know what this man's limitations were? Did God send him realizing the weaknesses but also having a use for the strengths of this man? Did God send the pastor expecting us to be able to build the Kingdom with him? Have we been assuming that we are finally the ones to please instead of God?

How do we feel about our fellow members in the congregation? Do we spend a lot of time griping about the organist, complaining about Sunday school teachers, or being negative about the youth group counselors? Do we just complain about members in general? But who brought us together? Wasn't it the Triune God, in whose name they were baptized? Isn't it our heavenly Father who saw fit to call them into our congregation by His Word? Don't we ask the Holy Spirit to govern all its activities, even the picking of people to fill the many roles?

When we start to think about it, we've all been brought together not so much by our idea as by God's. The dictionary says that complaining is "giving expression to resentment or grief at an undesirable situation." Has God created an undesirable situation in our community — the congregation? Our Lord Christ would go even deeper into discussing our particular congregation. He would say that not only was this His idea but that we are all members of His body on earth; we are part of one another. We find ourselves joined to the others as a result of His work. So there's not much point in analyzing the value of the other person. That would be like an eye saying to the toe of your body, "I don't need you." The body is there, and we don't discuss whether or not it ought to be a body.

Rather, assuming it is a body, we try to keep it as healthy as possible. When one member of the body shows weakness, the task is to help make it strong for everyone's sake. It's hard to imagine a Christian congregation that isn't bringing the best out of every member instead of griping about the worst. It's hard to imagine because Christ is so directly involved and we are so much a part of one another. It's hard to imagine a Christian family that doesn't regularly pray for its pastor and teachers and fellow members. They need it, and the family is surely interested in the best functioning of the body.

Our congregation isn't just another club in the area. It is the very body of our Lord Jesus Christ on earth. And He is right now standing at the door ready to take His body to Himself. What an exciting life it is to be all of us joined together in Christ, strengthening one another, praying for one another, working with one another, ready to meet our Head and hear from Him any comments about our work!

So let's talk:

Let's talk about our pastor and teachers.

Let's talk about "the way they do things" in our congregation.

Let's talk about the leaders of our congregation.

Now let's pray:

Our Father in heaven, we accept Your wisdom in calling us together into our congregation. We know You didn't call us because of our perfection but because of Your grace. Now forgive us for complaining about one another, and fill us with a realization of our oneness in Christ that we may support one another and so glorify You.

Patience

For our example of the patient endurance of suffering we can take the prophets who have spoken in the Lord's name. Remember that it is usually those who have patiently endured to whom we accord the word "blessed." You have heard of Job's patient endurance and how God dealt with him in the end, and therefore you have seen that the Lord is merciful and full of understanding pity for us men. James 5:10, 11

Teen-age is hardly the age of patience. In fact, nothing is more disguisting than to hear that ever-recurrent, "Wait and see. It all takes time." So James sounds like an old man when he encourages us to be patient. It's interesting, though, that James probably died as a young man and that there's nothing to indicate he was especially calm. What could he mean by patience?

We go off to high school, and it seems there's much in our Christianity to be impatient about. Why doesn't it have more answers? If Jesus is everyone's Redeemer, what about the natives who haven't heard of Him? If God is Ruler over all, why the mess in world affairs? If I am supposed to be a new creature in Christ, how come I don't feel that way? And so frequently the people we turn to don't give us much help. "You shouldn't ask," they seem to imply, or, "If you really believed, you wouldn't have those problems." Then we begin to be impatient with them. Surely they don't see the really basic issues of life. They've been too protected or too unwilling to think!

Or we become impatient with the "discipline" of our faith. Why must we keep going to church every Sunday? Why does everyone get so excited about Bible reading and daily devotions? After all, what good does it do? The rest of the crowd seems to be having a perfectly exciting time without all this stuff. Why must I be different? What does God expect of me anyway? Must I be some kind of saint? We wish we weren't expected to do so many things.

Here's where James would have some strong talk about patience, or endurance.

When Christ called the first disciples to Himself, He laid it right on the line. What He was doing wasn't going to make sense to men, but it was going to make sense to God. It wasn't men, after all, who had analyzed the world situation and pronounced it the result of sin. It was God. Nor was it men who had decided on the answer. When Christ therefore began to call people to Himself, He didn't begin to carefully explain all the minute details of God's thinking and work. That wasn't the great need. The great need was to proclaim Himself as God's answer to men. He spent His time revealing the will and plan of God, not *proving* it. The response to Him was one of faith. Those who believed in Him accepted His revelation. Those who rejected His Word wouldn't have believed under any circumstances. The disciples believed because they had been changed by the Holy Spirit. The challenge of their lives was to use that faith until they reached heaven, the completion of their journey. The testings and questions of men made them first of all call up their faith.

So an essential characteristic of a Christian disciple is endurance. Did Christ die on that cross? Did He die there for me? Will He keep His promises? These are the basic questions of faith. These the disciple can answer with certainty. He has that certainty as a gift of God. And because he has it, he can face all the problems one at a time. They are a matter of endurance, and endurance is one of the thrills he's ready to experience. "It is . . . those who have patiently endured to whom we accord the word 'blessed.'"

So let's talk:

> Is teen-age a special time of testing for Christian disciples?
>
> What are the biggest problems?
>
> What keeps parents, pastors, teachers from being more helpful?
>
> What in us is "impatience" instead of "endurance"?

A prayer suggestion:

Our Father in heaven, we know that we are not promised a crown with no cross, yet we usually don't want as lowly a cross as enduring patiently for You. Give us the grace to accept You and to let Your Spirit guide us through all the changes and problems of life; in Christ, our Lord.

Swearing

It is of the highest importance, my brothers, that your speech should be free from oaths (whether they are "by" heaven or earth or anything else). Your yes should be a plain yes, and your no a plain no, and then you cannot go wrong in the matter. James 5:12

James assumes that a Christian disciple is different from the ordinary person. He assumes that we are in fact people redeemed from a drab life of sin that we may live to the glory of God. He assumes further that this change permeates everything about us and that matters deemed unimportant to another person are "of the highest importance" to us.

Take the matter of oaths. Now, the ordinary person would say that an oath is a good thing, that it establishes truth. The ordinary person also gives no real heed to all those thoughtless phrases that dot our speech, like "by God," or "I'll swear on a stack of Bibles." It's just a part of the language.

But the disciple of Christ realizes that *any* oath is a tragedy. It's a tragedy because it demonstrates that we aren't the "image of God." The mere fact that a man must swear in court, for instance, is in effect an admission that pure truth can be established for only a moment or two under severe pressure. We can't just assume that men — God's people — are truthful all the time as part of their responsibility to Him. So even though there are times when he must swear to establish the truth, the disciple does it with a sense of sadness. To think that the image of God would fall into this kind of disrepair!

But if taking any oath is already tragedy, then the constant spouting of all kinds of silly oaths should be completely foreign to Christ's disciple. It makes no difference if it's "by" heaven or the Bible or anything else. To swear like this is an indication that we are not speaking or acting responsibly. If my heart is converted, my tongue will be converted along with it, and thoughtless swearing is completely inconsistent with what I am.

More self-discipline is called for. Isn't it true that too many Christians operate with a "What can I get by with?" approach to life? The big question is always: Is it wrong? The implication is that I would like to do this and hope that I will be permitted to get by with it. But such thinking implies that I am still unconverted, that I still feel the same about things. The word "discipline" goes with "disciple." A disciple is one who has a new approach to life, one that makes him change his habits, attitudes, actions. What has happened inside him must take form on the outside. The disciple gladly accepts this challenge and lets what has happened in his heart become a force in his actions. This is his "discipline."

So a disciple's tongue is a disciplined tongue, not because he's scared of the results of saying certain words but because he has come under the lordship of Jesus Christ. The disciple is accepting the challenge to let that lordship influence everything about him. The question is not so much: May people say this? as rather: May *I* say it? Is it consistent with what I am? And to be consistent it would have to be to the glory of God. Words are powerful, and the disciple uses them responsibly. It's pretty easy to see why both James and his Master would conclude that it is better to speak with plain words and not practice the embellishments of swearing or cursing. "Your yes should be a plain yes, and your no a plain no, and then you cannot go wrong in the matter."

So let's talk:

What do we consider "slang"?

What do we consider "swearing"?

Do we accept the responsibility of disciplined words?

What changes would be good in my speech habits?

A prayer suggestion:

Lord Jesus Christ, You have given us both the ability and the example for our life of discipleship. We confess that often words mean nothing to us, even words that are offensive to You. Forgive our lack of obedience and discipline, and fill us with the desire to be like You so that we may glorify You in our speech.

Praying in Trouble

If any of you is in trouble, let him pray. James 5:13

Should there be any need to tell us to pray when we are in trouble? Everyone does! In fact, some people pray only when they are in trouble. There are, however, some important aspects of praying in trouble that we ought to consider.

For one thing, how many prayers in trouble are just last-ditch efforts to make something happen? We have to turn somewhere, so we turn to God. Now, it's true that the depth of trouble can sometimes be the turning point in a person's life making his shout of help a call that continues into a new relation to God. But the person who is already Christian certainly will not be at that level of prayer. Or to put it another way, Christ's disciples will not wait for trouble to pray. There are other reasons for praying.

Furthermore, faith can be missing when we are praying in trouble. Many people pray with a sort of "Let's see what God will do about this" attitude. Two men prayed to Christ on the cross. One looked at the dying Figure and saw a King. He prayed for mercy from that King. The other said, "If You are the Son of God, save Yourself and us." He didn't believe that Jesus was God, and he figured this was God's chance to prove Himself. He was giving Him that chance! But God is not going to need trouble to prove that He is God. We cannot pray with a sort of challenge to God, "If You are God, then —" The issue of whether there is a God or not cannot be resolved in trouble. That should be settled before trouble comes.

Another problem is that our will and God's can clash in time of trouble. When we are in real trouble, there usually seems to be only one way out, and we know what it is. So we are in no position to be open to God's will. Yet the key to all of our life as God's children is that we look for His will and follow it. He has told us that His will is completely loving toward us. Trouble often tests our relation to that will. Prayer should have a prime place in trouble, but its place should be that of searching for God's will and the Holy Spirit.

So Jesus Christ alone can make us able to pray in trouble. After all, it is He who turns our hearts and minds to God with or without trouble. The person who has come to be one of His followers knows already where God fits in his life. Trouble will not change that. It will rather remind him immediately of where to turn. And it is Jesus Christ who takes our will captive to God's. That's the heart of our repentance, that we who were interested only in ourselves are now striving to follow God's will. In trouble we will continue to follow Him and to look for His will. And it is in Jesus Christ that we can live under God's will. In His "trouble" on earth He completely bowed to His Father's will and set Himself to follow it. So Christ gives the power, the ability, and the example for prayer.

Christians call upon God in the day of trouble; He will deliver them and they will glorify Him.

So let's talk:

Talk about the problem of praying *only* in trouble.

Talk about the problem of praying in trouble *without believing*.

Talk about the problem of *not being open to God's will* in trouble.

A prayer suggestion:

Our Father in heaven, we thank You for sending us Jesus Christ, through whom we have become Thy children and so are able to pray. Grant us Your Holy Spirit that we may pray at all times, not just when trouble brings us to You, and that when we are in trouble we may come in full assurance of faith.

Praise

If anyone is flourishing, let him sing praises to God. James 5:13

When James talks about "swearing," he adds some terse advice about how to express strong feelings. If we are in trouble, he suggests praying. If we are full of joy we should sing praises. If Christianity is discipleship and not just a cold set of propositions, then our feelings are certainly going to be important. After all, we are people — people with feelings as well as ideas, and these feelings are to be expressed.

But the measure of our discipleship is in the way we come to God with our joy, not just with our sorrow. A disciple is full of life, and so full of it that he can't help feeling the impact of being God's child. When things are going badly, he can't help coming to his Father to speak about it. But when things are going beautifully, he can't help using this cheerful spirit to offer up his praises to God, his Father.

After all, what else is man for? Didn't God create us that He might have someone with whom to share love? God certainly didn't need a manager to run the earth for Him. He knew what to do with His creation. Nor did He need us to help Him. He is almighty. But God needed us and made us because He wanted someone with whom to have fellowship. He built man for just this purpose. Can we imagine even the smartest animal having feelings of love and friendship? Can we imagine even the nicest tree being able to appreciate God and His work? Can we imagine any other creature than man writing a symphony or composing a psalm?

The truth of the matter is that we are God's children in creation, brought forth by God to be His own family on earth, able to love Him, able to receive His love, able to understand Him and to express our appreciation with words, thoughts, and feelings. God made us in His image. That means God made us to be like Him that we might be His "family" on this earth. True, man's sinfulness has ruined this part of his life, but we have been renewed in Christ to this kind of ability. "The eyes of all wait upon Thee, O Lord, and Thou givest them their meat in due season." That's certainly true, but only a new man in Christ could make the statement!

So how God must enjoy our moments spent praising Him! This is really the highest form of service we can give to God. How about the many hours a church choir spends trying to get a piece of music just right? Surely they aren't doing it to impress some people in church. Surely they are doing it to praise their Father. And how He must listen with joy in His heart at the labors they are going through *just for Him!* And what about the teen-agers gathered around a campfire singing their songs and saying their sentence prayers? Surely they are trying to express some of their feelings to God. And how He must enjoy their attempts to do it!

Praise is the keynote of a Christian life. It's hard to imagine a Christian devoting a week to God if he hasn't begun that week worshiping the Father. Nor can we think of a life of discipleship that isn't full of God and therefore full of praise for Him. "Oh, that I had a thousand voices to praise my God with thousand tongues!" is hardly a necessary wish. To what extent do I praise Him with the one tongue I have?

So let's talk:

How much praise shows up in my life?

What keeps me from praising Him more?

To what extent is public worship praise?

Let's pray:

We praise You, O Father, for all that You are and have done in our lives. We thank You for creating us in Your own image, that we might enjoy Your fellowship and return our feelings to You. We thank You especially for restoring Your image in us through our Savior's cross. Help us ever to express our cheerfulness in praise to You; through Christ, our Lord.

Sickness and Prayer

If anyone is ill, he should send for the church elders. They should pray over him, anointing him with oil in the Lord's name. Believing prayer will save the sick man; the Lord will restore him, and any sins that he has committed will be forgiven.
James 5:14, 15

How glad I am that my faith is mature enough to go beyond church services! How glad I am that it permeates everything about me and prompts me to live my whole life for God and my Savior!

There's sickness, for example. How completely lost and helpless a person feels lying there depending on others, counting on some pills, and anxious about his recovery! Sickness could be a mighty defeating experience. But look what resources I have as a disciple of Christ!

I have the resource of prayer. It's as simple as knowing that God hears prayers. The sick people who came to Jesus did not have to work out intricate reasons for coming or establish proof that they deserved help. They just knew that Jesus was God and that He had the complete power of life and health in His grasp. And they knew that He would listen, for they had found Him to be a loving, merciful person, ready to help those who came for it. So they came and asked, and He heard them. I am no different from them, and Jesus is no different today. I can come and ask for help in my sickness. I can actually help the doctor and the pills because I can ask Jesus to fill physician and medicine with His power. I can pray!

I have the resource of God's comfort. In the days of the Old Testament a sick person would send for the priest, and the priest would pour oil over him as he prayed. The oil was a concrete symbol of the pouring out of God's Spirit on a person. Imagine what the sick person must have thought as he felt the oil on his body: "God is that close to me and is pouring out His Spirit on me." It must have been a great source of strength to be so completely reminded of the nearness of God. Today the nearness of God is symbolized in another way. I can call for my pastor. As he comes to pray at my bedside, the nearness of God is somehow more concrete for me. As he says words which I am perhaps too weak or too discouraged to speak, I remember the protection of God and can take confidence in it. I have the comfort of God's protection.

I have the resource of forgiveness. Somehow when I'm sick, sin often bothers me. As I lie there depressed because of the interruption of my activities, worried about what will happen to me, I begin to wonder about my life and its many ups and downs. There's no getting around it, there are plenty of features in my life that make me quite uncomfortable. I begin to think that maybe I deserve a lot worse. But then I remember God's forgiveness. God doesn't intend to give me what I deserve. If He intended to treat me as a sinner, He wouldn't have sent Christ to face all the agony and suffering of the cross. As a matter of fact, God intends to do just the opposite. He has forgiven my sins in Christ so that I can have His life, and He will eventually take me right to His very side in heaven. Not what I may deserve but what God intends — that's the beauty of it all. What a joy to remember that God has forgiven me and will keep me as His child! I have the assurance of forgiveness.

Sickness is sad, and it can be fearful. But when I am sick, I will draw completely on my resources. I will send for my pastor, I will look into my Bible, I will talk to my fellow disciples. Behind them all is God, the Source of all my strength!

So let's talk:

Talk about some sickness and what it has meant.

A prayer suggestion:

Our Father in heaven, we thank You not only for saving us from death but also for keeping watch over us day by day. Help us remember You and Your almighty love when we are sick, that we may cheerfully accept Your will and faithfully pray for Your blessing, in Christ, our Lord.

Admitting Sins to One Another

You should get into the habit of admitting your sins to one another and praying for one another, so that if sickness comes to you you may be healed. James 5:16

Let's say that James addressed this sentence to our family. Could we actually take it seriously? It isn't easy to imagine mother or father admitting sins to sons and daughters. Nor does it seem possible for a teen-ager to let his folks know what his sins happen to be. We would want to know of what great value it might be before we tried anything so radical as confessing our sins to one another.

So we start with Christ. His mission on earth was to "save us from our sins." There's good reason for saying "our sins." We have done them, and many times they continue to be part of us long after they were first committed. Either they trouble our consciences, or they become a habit and continue to bother us. Being "saved" from them is a good deal more concrete than a simple statement that Christ died for them a long time ago. Something more personal needs to happen with the specific sins we commit.

That's why Christ wasn't content simply to die and ascend back to heaven. Before He left this earth, He made provision for that concrete, practical, personal dealing with our sins. While He was on earth, He could say to a sinner, "Your sins are forgiven," and the sinner could go away happy because Jesus had told him that *his* sins were forgiven — the specific sins which he had told Him. When Jesus was getting ready to return to His Father's home, He made provision for this kind of forgiving to continue. "Receive the Holy Ghost," He said. "If you forgive any man's sins, they are forgiven; and if you hold them unforgiven, they are unforgiven." He endowed His disciples with the authority to speak for Him. They were to be His representatives on earth, and as such they had full rights to speak for Him. The Holy Spirit living in them made them able to show people the way to God just as Christ had done. He also made them able to deal with sins just as Christ had done. Naturally it's a delegated authority and has the limitations of such delegation, but it's a bona fide authority nevertheless.

So every Sunday morning when we confess our sins at the beginning of the service, it's no mere ceremony when the minister says: "As a called and ordained servant of the Word I announce the grace of God unto all of you, and in the stead and by the command of my Lord Jesus Christ I forgive. . . ." He is the one who has been called by

Christ to do this publicly in this congregation for all the people present.

But the minister's work is always the public exercise of a responsibility that every Christian is to exercise daily. A minister preaches on Sunday morning, but every Christian bears witness to Christ in his daily contacts with men. The Gospel is given to each of us to speak to other people. When people respond to that Gospel, we are given the responsibility of assuring them that their sins are forgiven. So James must surely have ordinary Christians in mind when he encourages us to "get into the habit of admitting your sins to one another and praying for one another." This confessing to one another and praying for one another is normal Christian activity.

And what does it accomplish? It accomplishes the basic plan of Christ, that people should have a personal, concrete, specific opportunity to be "saved" from their sins. He died to do the saving. But now I need a good opportunity to lay these sins down and walk off from them. As I actually tell them to another Christian, I am very specifically laying them down in front of Christ, and as I actually *say* I am sorry, I am dealing with them specifically. When my fellow Christian tells me I am forgiven, this sends me on my way knowing that the very sins I talked about are forgiven. And what has been the result for one another? We have come closer to one another in the bonds of Christ. Love, acceptance, understanding — all become meaningful words because they are what is happening while we are confessing sins and praying for one another.

So let's talk:

> Is it really possible for our family to confess sins to one another?
>
> What are the greatest obstacles?
>
> What changes will we have to make?

What value will it have for the person confessing?

What value will it have for our family?

A prayer suggestion:

Lord Jesus Christ, we are completely overpowered when we realize what You have done in letting us speak forgiveness to one another. Give our family the ability to use this precious privilege to the strengthening of each member and the building up of our home as a dwelling place for You.

What Can Prayer Do?

Tremendous power is made available through a good man's earnest prayer. Do you remember Elijah? He was a man like us, but he prayed earnestly that it should not rain. In fact, not a drop fell on the land for three and a half years. Then he prayed again; the heavens gave the rain, and the earth sprouted with vegetation as usual. James 5:16-18

Does prayer change things? Never! The point we're trying to make is simple: Too many people put their faith in prayer instead of in God. There exists a sort of folk-religion which makes a twin god out of faith and prayer. We hear the songs and read the success stories of what power there is in believing and what "prayer can do." But what the person believes is unimportant so long as it is sincere. And prayer is a sort of magic button that has no real connection with God or His will. Just faith and prayer, these are the essentials of being religious, according to this kind of thinking.

The essential of religion is God, His personality, His will, His power. All our "religious exercises" and confidences revolve around Him, or they are ridiculous. Jesus Christ didn't come into the world to make men better "pray-ers" or believers in something — they certainly were good enough at that. He came to show them the Father and to bring them back before Him. So prayer by itself is nothing more than the words or wishes of a person. Elijah's story certainly shows how useless prayer can be. The prophets of Baal prayed and prayed and prayed to Baal for fire. Nothing happened.

But God is able and willing to change things. He makes it very clear in our Scriptures that He is Lord of the entire universe and yet is concerned with the smallest sparrow. He is very much involved in life. And in His involvement He invites us to pray, to bring Him our requests. He has given us enough examples to encourage our prayers too. Abraham prayed for Lot's family, and God spared them. Moses prayed for Israel, and God did not destroy the nation. When Peter was in prison, the whole church prayed earnestly through the night, and Peter was set free. There are plenty of encouraging examples of what can happen when we pray; they show us what God can do! And God has put the examples down in writing to encourage us to do the same thing.

But even more encouraging to us is what our Lord Jesus Christ has done. He sums up His ministry frequently in relation to our prayers. He shows us that though we on our part are undeserving of any hearing, He has reconciled us to the Father. We thus come to Him as sons and not as enemies. He further points out that we may come to the Father with all our concerns because the Father loves us. He sees His death on the cross as the breaking down of any separation between us and the Father so that we have no barrier to our prayers. In fact, "whatsoever you shall ask the Father in My name." We might say that the real climax of Jesus' work for us is our ability to pray to the Father, unhindered in any way. It reaches its peak when He teaches us to pray, "Our Father. . . ."

Jesus therefore wants us to pray. We who are His disciples bear a special relation to the world: we can pray for it to the Father. The New Testament shows us that the exercise of our faith includes the bringing of this world's need to the Father in prayer. "I exhort that first of all prayers should be made for all men, for kings. . . ." While others plan and ponder, we can pray. While others despair and fail, we can bring the needs to God. Tremendous power is made available through a good man's prayer: the power of God. We who are Christ's bear the responsibility of praying for all men.

So let's talk:

> Talk about how significant Christians can be in world crises.
>
> Talk about what we've prayed about in the last month.
>
> Talk about the prayers of our congregation.
>
> Talk about people we should be praying for.

Prayer:

Lord Jesus Christ, we thank You for making it possible for us to pray. Enable us now to fully use this privilege, that coming to our Father in full confidence we may lay our requests before Him, seeking to accomplish His will.

Precious Sinners

My brothers, if any of you should wander away from the truth and another should turn him back onto the right path, then the latter may be sure that in turning a man back from his wandering course he has rescued a soul from death, and his loving action will "cover a multitude of sins." James 5:19, 20

What a way to end a letter! There are no personal greetings or instructions as with the other letters of the New Testament. We find no conclusive summary. This is just the abrupt emphasis on how precious one sinner is and how important it is to save that one person. Was James cut off in his writing, or does he have a deliberate reason for stopping? Couldn't it be that this *is* the real conclusion to the whole matter? Isn't it true that James has in so many ways been indicating the preciousness of a person's life? Hasn't he been saying that it is so precious that no sacrifice is really too much? And isn't he now wanting to end by directing us to cultivate that precious attitude to other people?

Every person is precious. Imagine a little child fallen into a deep, dry well. What a stir to save him! Huge machines come crashing across the lawns to the spot. Volunteers begin digging on hourless shifts, and no possible effort is overlooked. The heroic crusade continues even when there is no hope left that the child is still alive. We just wouldn't feel right if we didn't do everything we could regardless of the chances. That's how precious a little child is, and none of us would begrudge a penny of the expense or a minute of the work. We just don't say, "Well, it's only one person! Forget it!"

God made us that precious, "for God made man in His image." Even though man lost this image because of his sin, God spared no effort to save us from death. For Christ to enter this world, to be abused by the mobs, to hang in pain on the cross was a tremendous sacrifice, but He didn't begrudge men one moment of it. That's how precious we were in His sight. For Him to take His time to call down the little crook Zacchaeus and actually visit His home was no burdensome effort. Zacchaeus was precious. In fact, Jesus would have us understand that the host of angels in heaven break into song when a sinner repents; that's how happy everyone around God's throne is over one precious person's salvation.

So there we are. Do we share any of that enthusiastic willingness? After all, isn't the church on earth God's rescue squadron? One of the old symbols of the church is that of a ship, for like a ship it rescues all kinds of sinners from the threatening waters. It stands to reason that the ship can't be permanently docked in some safe harbor. Yet the church is made up of people like us. Its attitudes are finally the sum total of *our* attitudes, and its interest or lack of interest will reflect how much *we* are concerned.

Yet how quickly we lose this feeling for the preciousness of people. If it's only one friend we've hurt, we are glad for the friends we've kept. So there's one fellow Christian who seems to be drifting out of the group and isn't seen around anymore. At least most of them are still faithful. How far we fall from Jesus' illustration about a man leaving 99 sheep behind to look for one lost one! It's probably easier to go and win two more than to bring the lost back. And then we'll have our hundred again — and one extra. Satan would have us constantly play down the preciousness of one person. It's his way of destroying God's people.

We need the mind of Christ. The Christ whose heart went out to the floundering Judas, whose eye fell on the widow who had just lost her only son, who grieved inwardly when a young man decided not to follow Him — He needs to fill us with the same feeling for people. And with that mind we need to look for the straying ones all around us, in our congregation, among our friends, down our street — those precious people who need to be rescued. Yes, this is the place to leave James but not before asking ourselves how precious each individual is to us.

So let's talk:

How precious are people to me?
How precious are sinners to my congregation?
Which precious ones am I ignoring?

Let's pray:

Forgive us our cold hearts, O Lord Jesus; forgive us our unsearching eyes; forgive us our unwilling hands; forgive us our lazy lips; forgive us our reluctant feet; forgive us for letting Your precious people go unrescued and for being interested only in ourselves. Warm our hearts, open our eyes, move our lips, lift our feet by the power of Your Holy Spirit that we may bring back sinners from their ways and thus cover vast multitudes of sins.